GARLIC FOR PEGASUS

GARLIC FOR PEGASUS

The Life of Brother Benito de Goes
of the Society of Jesus

by Wilfred P. Schoenberg, S. J.

THE NEWMAN PRESS · WESTMINSTER, MARYLAND
1955

Imprimi potest: Harold O. Small, S.J.
Provincialis Praepositus Provinciae Oregoniensis

Nihil obstat: Joannes J. Coleman, J.C.D.
Censor Librorum

Imprimatur: ✠ Carolus D. White,
Episcopus Spokanensis

die 23 mensis Octobris, 1954

To

OUR LADY OF THE SNOWS

ON WHOSE NAME-DAY

THIS WORK WAS BEGUN

PREFACE

"PEGASUS," I would have you know, was the winged horse seen most often over the mythical mountains of ancient Greece. He still lives —over certain service stations; I forget now which kind. You've noticed him there, a lithe, sleek, red horse with graceful wings.

Garlic plays a major role in the adventures of our Pegasus. Were it not for garlic (at least so Brother de Goes assures us), the beast would long since have died (in 1603), and I suppose the service stations would have had to employ another symbol.

How de Goes used garlic to sustain life in Pegasus is part of the story. Just a part. But it seems to me it epitomizes the Jesuit Brother's epic journey in one idea: a trip by horse across the "Roof of the World" under the most hazardous conditions imaginable. It can serve, then, as a key-concept for us. It can illustrate an adventurous life, all of which was intense, but never more so than on the "Roof of the World," where Pegasus, Garlic, and de Goes formed an everlasting alliance.

The amazing part of the de Goes story is that it is true. It actually happened; and this biography is authentic to the extent that critical works on the subject have been carefully followed—in some instances, verbatim. As is plainly evident, I have taken certain liberties in the hope of reconstructing scenes and dialogues more naturally. When sources differed among themselves on minor points I felt free, without further research, to use that view which more aptly served my purpose.

It is a pleasant duty to record my obligations to others. I am greatly indebted to my superiors, Father Harold O. Small, S.J. and Father Hilary Werts, S.J., for their help and encouragement. Many others were of service, generously and unstintingly, and while it would be impractical to record them all by name, I cannot fail to mention several: Father Edward Hagemann, S.J., who gave me much needed aid with sources; Father Carl Twaddell, S.J., for valued advice and illustrations; Father John Perlite, S.J., for the map used as end-sheets; Fathers John P. Leary, S.J. and Russell M. Boehning, S.J., who helped me in many different ways.

I also wish to express my appreciation to The Macmillan Company for their kind permission to use material from my essay, "Gypsy Come Home," in *Better A Day* (1951), edited by John P. Leary, S.J.

WILFRED P. SCHOENBERG, S.J.

ALMA, CALIFORNIA
Candlemas Day, 1952

viii

CONTENTS

PART **1** ● THE TUNIC

I

THE YEAR 1583 was not a particularly momentous one. At least it was not marked by a great famine or that other curse called conquest. It was just another hour in the Golden Age of the Iberian Peninsula, of Spain and Portugal, who had inherited the Mediterranean's lost glory and together sifted the world for its spoils, the one by ruling and the other by trading.

No one had effectively challenged either. That is, not until the English, disdainfully called "Luteranos" by the Spaniards, scurried about the seas in lady-like pinnaces and just for the joy of it sniped at the lordly Iberian galleons.

Elizabeth, their queen, knighted them for this piracy! Many another Christian ruler would have hanged such petty outlaws from the nearest yardarm. According to Spain, which clung to its lofty perch and loudly proclaimed its sovereignty over land and sea, time and God would manifest the futility of this English impudence.

Not without point, for indeed Spain ruled vast stretches of the world, or had at least explored its farthest corners; but the cost in manpower, ships, and production was inevitably beginning to tell. Spanish villages had been emptied of their youth to fill chairs of colonial administration far across the seas. The Spanish economy, flattened by dropping gold values and increasing taxation, groaned behind the façade of political glory. The expulsion of the thrifty Moriscos (who fled to prosper in England and Flanders) forever crippled Spain's productivity. In 1583 the Golden Era still shone resplendently, but the glitter was not to last very much longer.

If Spain was bleeding itself out by populating ever-expanding frontiers, Portugal was no less following the same suicidal path. "I am dying with my country," were among the last words of Camoes, one of the greatest Portuguese poets, and his ominous reflection proved to be startlingly accurate.

Portugal's days were indeed numbered. Death was in the body, and there was no physician to prescribe remedies. Had one been at hand, he would have said the heart was too small for the portly body. Tiny Portugal was simply breaking down under the strain of pumping energy into a vast empire. Meanwhile the flag of Portugal, with Spanish approval, waved in such distant places as Brazil and the East Indies. The tiny Iberian kingdom spread its soldiers over that half of the globe it had been expediently granted by the Borgia Pope in 1493.

Assuredly these far-flung armies afforded some measure of protection for the Jesuit missionaries who preceded or followed or accompanied them to heathen shores; but by and large the ambassadors of Christ would gladly have been done with their Portuguese guardians of law and order. Like some occupation forces in our own time, they bullied the natives and stole their petty valuables and seduced their pretty maidens. This was not true of all of the soldiers, of course, but the majority had been sired by an evil age, and were either too ignorant to know better, or too weakened by example to take the other course.

With the Jesuit missionaries it was a totally different affair. They had not come ten thousand miles in stinking, leaky boats to compete with their compatriots in the mad game of money or conquest. They had come to serve God, and that was much harder than gathering money—but was infinitely more satisfying. The Jesuits concentrated on Asia's sub-continent, or rather the fringe of it, for the very simple reason that the fringe gave them plenty to do. Besides, the interior was beyond the reach of the foreigner, whatever his objective. And somewhere in that interior was something very mysterious, something that Europe had read and heard about, had once been in contact with, but had long since lost. Somewhere in Asia was the answer to a lost empire, Cathay.

The legends which grew up around Cathay began with the travels of Marco Polo in the thirteenth century. Marco, with his father and uncle, had penetrated far to the east of Europe. The three of them, wide-eyed adventurers from Venice, had audaciously walked into the capital city of Cathay, Cambaluc, or "Khan's Town." Here for seventeen years Marco had served as Kublai Khan's errand boy and man of parts, a post which enabled him to study Mongolian dominions at close range. For the Khan he treaty'd and traded, and above all remembered. Then, like the typical European abroad, he hankered for his homeland and returned to Italy. Genoa, which was at war with Venice, clapped him into its jailhouse, where he told his whopping tale. Rustigielo di Pisa put it in writing.

Soon all Europe was devouring it. Cambaluc and Cathay became as famous as Constantinople and Alexandria. Cathay grew into the fabulous land of silks and slant-eyed writers who used brushes to paint several words in a single character. Pope Clement V caught the fever and dispatched Friar John, a Franciscan, as Archbishop of Cambaluc. Friar John's mission prospered till at eighty-two he died and was buried with great pomp.

No one took his place, because the hospitable Mongols were ousted by the Mings of China and Cathay was lost forever. For centuries Europeans schemed to return to this land of silks. Dreamers dreamed. Liars invented. Geographers made maps. But Cathay was a Lost Empire, as surely buried as Homer's Troy.

The geographer Christopher Columbus was an heir to all this romance. And Columbus cherished his own dream: he would rediscover this lost kingdom. The world (of course) was round and he, Christopher Columbus, would kiss Cathay's shores by sailing west. "To Cathay!" he cried, and "To Cathay!" cried all his men, his sailors and alley-thugs. They set sail to the west and stumbled upon that most inconsiderate periphery of a dark unknown continent which was to be named America. Columbus died. The explorers who came after him, fellow-Bohemians of the sea-ways who had profited from his experiences, continued the search.

In the course of time and fortune, Portugal's banners drew closer to the region of Marco Polo's diplomacy. Where, the Portuguese asked, is Cathay? No Cathay? China, they were told. China and Peking and Canton, but no Cathay. So the land-hunt dragged on.

Jesuits, meanwhile, fell under the spell of the mystery too. Francis Xavier had heard of Cathay. He died in the very shadow of its unfriendly shores without recognizing it. Before another century had passed, the salt-waves washed the bones of a hundred Jesuits who had left

Europe behind them, hope high in their hearts that they would reclaim the lost Christians of Cathay. But still they came, undaunted by the fate of their predecessors. Among these newcomers was Father Matthew Ricci.

If Francis Xavier was a Moses, who died with eyes cast on forbidden land, Ricci the Jesuit was Joshua. For him Cathay was the Promised Land and he entered it openly, almost brazenly. He used clocks and geometry to do it, and he soon found himself an honored guest beneath the emperor's roof in Nanking.

From Nanking, Ricci wrote startling news. Cambaluc was Cambaluc, but it was also Peking; and Cathay was China! He had come to this conclusion, he explained, by studying Marco Polo's descriptions of thirteenth-century Cathay. Seventeenth-century China tallied perfectly with Polo's account and he felt there was little, if any, reason to doubt that he was right.

"Could this be true?" Jesuits were asking one another. "How could pagan China be Christian Cathay?" Impossible. Ricci's opinion was openly questioned and the mythical land grew mistier than ever.

In particular, the Jesuits in India paid little heed to "good Father Matthew." He was a crack mathematician, they said. Let him look to that. For their part they felt assured that a vast kingdom peopled with anxious Christians lay between India and China. Some day they would prove it.

At this point an amazing person entered upon the scene. He was a Jesuit brother, Portuguese by birth, and missionary in India by preference. His name was Benito de Goes.

Benito de Goes had left the Azores when he was too young to know better. The whole world was his oyster, not nine small islands eight hundred miles from the coast of Portugal. So it was the world he set out to claim.

But fortune, whose favors are for the few, had not smiled. Benito, perhaps reluctantly, joined the colonial army and was swept over the seas in troop-ships. From port to port he shifted with the changing seasons, into the Persian Gulf where Portugal maintained a fortress, to Macao where Portuguese traders intrigued and plotted, to the Celebes, the Fishery Coast, Cochin, Malacca, where Portugal's flag flapped arrogantly against the blue, and hate smoldered beneath dark skins because that flag was there, and there, and everywhere else.

One day in 1583, de Goes was sent by military authorities to the Coast of Malanor. Of late he had been despondent. His unholy follies had brought no happiness and he was filled with such bitter remorse that he despaired of salvation from hell.

In this bankruptcy of soul and spirit he beached at Coleichi, a green little village of the Province of Travancore, which runs along the coast north and west of India's tip. Benito beat a hasty, boisterous departure from the ship with his companions, reserving his wit for good times, his wages for gaming, and his feet for dancing. More laughter, more slavery to convention (that demanding mistress), and then he would creep off to nurse his pain in solitude.

Near Coleichi a little church named for a lovely maid, the Virgin Mary, had been tucked beneath the palm trees. A residence for the Jesuit pastor stood near by. The steeple of Mary's dedication pointed into the skies, higher than the local mosque, high enough for sea-soldiers approaching the beach to discover it and know that there was God, there on a lonely India-coast.

God's own roof among the palm trees. Benito, a lad of twenty-two, saw it and his spirit trembled within him. What had God's roof to do with him this sultry afternoon when all nature spoke of ease and pleasure and bade him try once more? Happiness was in a cup, or in his noisy cards, or in just plain noise, but not in that silent Church beneath the palm trees.

Benito's heart followed pleasure, but his mind remained with God's house. It obsessed him. His coarse laughter became hollow, his song still, his wine all bitter. Had remorse poisoned it? Had God in His judgments already sentenced him? No, no! But the vision of God's roof remained, the roof of God's house. It possessed his soul and gave him no peace at all.

That night he dreamt of a criminal court where the judge wore black robes and a powdered wig and shook his finger angrily at the sinner—at all sinners. Why, the judge was God's house! The house stood up on legs, like a man, and it pulled the black robes about itself and pointed an incredibly long finger at him, at the sinner. God's house was judging him.

Well then, let God's house pass judgment. Let the sinner appear before it and hear his sentence. He raised himself wearily before the judge while a thousand questions plagued his mind and demanded resolving—did God's house have ears? Did God's house speak loudly, so that he would know what sentence had been passed? Did accusation lighten the sentence? And each question went

9

by unanswered, for God's house, weeping bitterly, said it could not render justice, but only mercy.

On the morning that followed, Benito screwed up his courage and made his way toward the church among the palm trees. From the outside it looked cold and hard to him, like unrelenting justice. He examined it nervously. He stood there a long time, summoning all the courage in his bones. A sound, an appearance, or even a breath of air could have frightened him off. He felt like a suicide just before the fatal plunge, only this was more difficult than suicide. One move, one self-determined act, would decide his fate.

Benito turned sharply to look into the road below him. One lone boy trotted along, wearing his near-nakedness gaily, his skin as brown as mahogany. He was making monkey sounds and laughing to himself that he could be so clever. Benito enviously watched him disappear among the coconut palms, then suddenly, with an impetuous shove, he opened the church door and crept through—God's house.

He stared furtively in all the dark corners, as if he expected demons to pop out and pounce upon him. His eyes sought out huddled old women, shawled denizens of the gloom, but there were none. Up to the main altar he crept with halting, bewildered steps. And then he fell on his knees.

After what seemed like endless hours, he looked up to the altar and saw a painting there, a painting of the Virgin with the divine Child on her lap. All the goodness of his childhood came back to him like a wave of bitter-sweet memories. His own mother's tenderness. His First Communion Day and the hymns that were sung. The *Aves* babbled beside his bed while his mother bent over him, sweetly waiting to kiss him good night.

10

Memories were too much for a lonely, heartsick lad far from home. He buried his head in his arms and wept like a child, as he really was. And while he wept, he looked up for a moment at the painting above him. The Virgin's eyes gazed down on him, most tenderly, he thought, and the Infant sat very still, very stiffly. But what was wrong? Benito looked closer and his heart stopped beating. The Infant was weeping too!

Half afraid lest he break the spell, Benito put his hand to the painting, and a tear fell on it, a milk-white tear clinging there to his finger. In a daze he turned around and hurried out. He wasn't sure. He couldn't be sure. He'd ask others to come and see; he'd ask his companions, if he could find them.

Still peering at his finger where the tear had fallen, he plunged down the road and through the palm trees.

III

In Coleichi that same morning, little João had met his own shattering crisis. João was an orphan boy whom the village had taken in. The Padri had fetched him in from the bush with the brusque remark, "His parents are dead." That was the Padri's way of saying, "Now he is ours. We will care for him."

The Padri had baptized him "João," a name which might have honored any one of a dozen saints. As a matter of fact, one of his descendants would be fabulously holy and a bishop besides. For the present, though, João was as normal in his piety as all the other "Joãos" christened by the Padri.

Like many young boys João was indifferent to the opinions of his elders. The elders, for example, didn't like

11

the snakes he brought home. Just why not, João couldn't say, for the long, slithering serpents fascinated him beyond all else. That is, except eating and fiestas.

This morning on his way to the river (where snakes were as fat as tree limbs) João hadn't even noticed the strange soldier glaring fiercely at him from the church door. In fact he hadn't noticed the church. In his blindness he had hopped along, chattering to himself, with nothing to worry about except, perhaps, where to find a club to use on the vipers. This was a kind of vacation time, because the Padri, who sometimes taught him letters, was far away at a mission station. The Padri, João remembered, was going to make him a catechist, whatever that was.

The boy was creeping along now, by the shallow lagoon, mumbling "Catechist, catechist, catechist" to himself. Quite suddenly, as if thunder had struck in a blue sky, he heard a volley of musket shot. Following that, there was the roar of many cannon, and then the birds about him fluttered nervously and let out plaintive little peeps. João was as frightened as the birds till he got an idea. "Fiesta?" he asked himself sharply. Had he forgotten a fiesta? Unthinkable, but what else could the booming be?

"A miracle! A miracle!" he heard when he finally emerged from the jungle. The boy wasn't sure what a miracle meant, but he would take care that he missed nothing.

"João, João, a miracle! Go see the miracle!" Rodrigo's old woman, blowzy and gray, shouted at him when she saw his nut-brown face. Her legs were too watery to carry her very far. "That's a good boy, João; go see the miracle. And come to my side to tell me in all truth."

The old woman knew a miracle when she saw it. Had

12

she not seen the great Xavier himself raise the dead to life? Those dead had been like Lazarus, entombed and stinking. It was at Coulan, up the coast a bit, about forty years ago. She ought to remember, because she was carrying Paolo then. She had heard of another miracle—Xavier had raised a widow's dead boy while mourners carried him to his grave. There was a holy one!

The guns continued to assert themselves and the old woman was goggling with curiosity. "Oh la!" she screamed with each booming echo, "a miracle!" She struggled to make her way up the road, but finally had to sit on the ground and peer at the church in the distance.

João's legs were ready to buckle when he caught up at last with the crowd. "A miracle! a miracle!" people were howling. To João it sounded like the huzzahs villagers roared when the ships blew in.

Was this the "miracle"? João stared at the women praying aloud with their arms outstretched. Others were kissing the ground and some were singing hymns with much noise and fervor. Candles appeared and a procession formed, even without the Padri.

Most incongruous of all were the soldiers. They were wildly running everywhere, whacking down saplings and ferns with their swords, piling them into the church.

"See," one shouted, holding up a tiny white rag, "this was dipped in the Infant's tears!" João looked at it stupidly, then into the soldier's face to see whether he was serious or not.

The soldier was. "I'll buy a candle," he vowed. "Three pounds." No one save João was listening. "I'll confess. I'll go back to my wife at Goa. I'll . . ." João turned to something more intelligible, a dog who had

13

lately joined the celebration wagging his tail with delirious joy.

The old woman, it turned out, finally got her story from Rodrigo.

"That picture in the church," he said, "it cried. I mean that the Baby cried while a soldier prayed."

At this point the old woman shook him soundly. She suspected he had been taking boiled wine again. One of his sailor friends smuggled it in—for the best in ivory. "Is that your miracle?" she demanded.

"It's the truth!" he swore. "Ask the Jew Jacobo."

"What's the truth?"

"That Baby in the church cried. I mean the Baby in the picture." He watched her wide, expansive face as if he were scanning the sky for storm signals. "While a soldier prayed—from the post," he waved his hand in the general direction of the Portuguese barracks, "the Baby cried out and he got his friends and they all saw it and one of them dipped his handkerchief into the white tears. Like milk." He nodded solemnly. "Then the Baby stopped crying."

"You mean the Baby in the picture?"

He nodded again.

"The one the Virgin holds?"

"That one."

"Oh la! a miracle! a miracle!" she screamed.

That night Rodrigo had the best dinner ever. João was right beside him, celebrating the miracle.

In subsequent weeks the villagers came to know "that soldier from the barracks" for what he was, as well as for what he had been. The new Benito was quite a contrast to the old, and Rodrigo's old woman had often remarked on it. Dedicated, like so many of her sex, to the cult of news, particularly that of a preter-

14

natural kind, she had lost no time in discovering the events that led up to the village "miracle." She had, perforce, got her story piece-meal, but for all that it lost none of its flavor. "Oh la!" she would begin, when passing it along, "I must tell you what else I heard today about this soldier de Goes." She noticed, with the rest of the villagers, that he spent most of his leisure time in church before the picture where the Infant had wept for him. This was a wonder in itself, almost a miracle, and the old woman loved it.

Benito's confreres at the barracks liked to tell new-comers that he went to church every time the bell rang, like an old woman who had little else to occupy her. Of course this was a joke, a soldier's exaggeration, but it took courage to withstand the guffawing that always accompanied it. "Why not be a monk!" some scoffed during countless discussions about his change of life. "Oh yes, do be a monk!"

Why not be a monk? Why not join an army of monks where one need not face ridicule to say one's prayers? Benito had been considering it for weeks. At first he didn't tell anyone, not even the Padri. In his own mind he weighed its advantages and disadvantages, and then he sought the Padri who had healed his ailing soul.

Yes, the Padri told him, it seemed that God was calling him to the Company of Jesus. Could he go to Goa where the Provincial lived? The Father Provincial would have to question him and consult others regarding the matter. Yes, by all means, go to Goa.

In February, 1584, Benito de Goes appeared at the Jesuit Professed House in Goa. He was quietly intro-duced to the Provincial, Father Alexander Valignano, the Jesuit rover of seven seas and organizer *par excellence* of the Society in India and Japan.

15

The two seated themselves in a stiff little parlor with many windows.

"You were born in Portugal?" the Father asked with a piercing glance. He had an eye as sharp as an eagle.

"In the Islands, Your Reverence. In the Azores on the Isle of Saint' Miguel. My village is Villa Franca de Campo."

"When was this?"

"1562, Your Reverence."

"You have been to school?" Valignano was making mental notes. The lad is too serious . . . mature for his age . . . some sorrow perhaps.

"Yes, Your Reverence."

"How long?"

"Several years." Benito recalled the hard benches, greatest of life's restraints, and the rude school master who posed as an aesthete from Lisbon.

"Tell me, Benito, why do you wish to join our Company rather than one of the older religious orders?"

Benito perked up, startled out of his reveries on school. Why did the Father ask a question like this? Was it, as he feared, that the Company had no place for sinners? "I made my general confession to one of your Fathers. I sought his advice. And I've heard of Father Francis Xavier—I really don't know. . . ." He regretted the lameness of his answer. What was the Father Provincial thinking—those eyes seemed to discover one's very thoughts before they were formed.

"Did this Father you spoke to persuade you to come to me?"

"He advised it, Your Reverence."

"Did he talk you into it, that's my point?" Father Valignano spread his fingers in a gesture of "Do-you-get me?" "You see, Benito, if anyone has urged or put pres-

16

sure on you to become a Jesuit, I cannot accept you as a candidate."

Benito said "No," no one had persuaded him.

"But why do you ask to be a Brother?"

Benito's brow puckered in distress. "I want to serve God in religion, Your Reverence, but I do not wish to take Holy Orders."

"Perhaps God calls you to Orders."

"No, Your Reverence, I do not think so. I merely wish to serve God in holy religion."

"Have you any dependents?"

"No, Your Reverence."

"Are you willing to go anywhere you are sent for the glory of God and the good of souls?"

"Anywhere, Reverend Father! Please give me a chance."

Benito was accepted for a two-and-a-half-year trial, during which time both the Provincial and Benito would make up their minds.

Father Valignano bent over his records to write telegraphically: "Benito de Goes. From the town of Villa Franca of the Azores, of the Diocese of Portugal, twenty-three years of age, robust in health, entered in the year 1584, in the month of February, assigned to household duties."

In a few hours Benito gathered his belongings and moved into a damp, drab building which four years before had been St. Rocque's Sanatorium. It was the Jesuit Novitiate.

IV

Brother de Goes was no swashbuckler of the cloister, like the Jesuits of fable. Because he was older than most of those in the Novitiate with him, he accepted the cloister's lessons more warily and with a measure of worldly skepticism. The others were eager and impetuous, like school-boys; he was more like a retired provincial lawyer who has taken himself to religion tardily, but with immense determination to polish up the soul for a final showdown.

The retired lawyer, when he passes into the monastic world, closes certain doors of his mind and tries desperately to open others. He keeps, after the manner of still worldly men, his own standards of excellence. He advances cautiously, though surely. Above all he is cautious in his hopes and in his speech.

In a way, caution was Brother de Goes' strength. It was also his weakness.

His companions said he was "quiet" (which for a novice means "patient"), and they would add to this the word "prudent." Patient and prudent, that was de Goes. All agreed that he was a notable. His easy manners betrayed a cultivated background and his judgment a just-as-highly developed mind. He had already mastered several languages with ready facility.

Superiors were so impressed by this blend of prudence and learning that they urged him several times to change his status.

"Study theology. Be a priest," they said.

"No," he firmly replied each time, and the matter was finally dropped.

18

It wasn't that the Superiors felt only dull and docile creatures should be lay-brothers. Quite the contrary. They were all familiar with the duke-turned-Brother cases common enough in a Catholic Europe. They knew a score of degree-men who scrubbed the kitchen kettles for the greater glory of God. Jesus Christ had sanctified manual labor for twenty-five years and nothing could diminish its splendor.

But Brother Benito, well, he was more like St. Paul than St. Francis of Assisi. St. Paul made a better priest and St. Francis a better Brother. Like Francis, however, Brother Benito had his own lights from heaven, and a Brother he remained. "It is my vocation," he would simply say and that was the end of it.

But as a "vocation" it was only a beginning. There must be a long, painful process before the soldier would be transformed into a Jesuit Brother, and Benito didn't half suspect the course it would take. He was perfectly willing to transform himself in his own way, even prepared to kill his spirit in the struggle. But what did happen caught him completely by surprise. He didn't know till ten years later that his was a characteristic experience, that God, when He takes over, acts quite contrary to all human anticipations.

To begin with, the novitiate itself was not what de Goes had expected. Just what it would have been had he designed it is hard to say. What he found, besides the damp, drab building, was that curse of the restless called "order." Monotony.

At first it was a relief from the turmoil he had known. Benito liked the calm and the hush. He liked the simple tasks assigned to him, helper to the cook, laundry man, companion for priests on their calls. He felt "holy" in his sacred surroundings; in fact, he tingled all over with "holiness" when the organ boomed at benediction or when he knelt at night in a chapel which was all dark save for the burning sanctuary light. Gladly would he dispense with food, sleep, even breathing, so that he could taste the longer these sensible consolations, this spiritual baby food.

But as the year passed by, things changed. Each day brushed a little off, till the novelty had all worn away and de Goes came to grips with his real self for the first time. Stripped now of his sensible consolations, he was caught between the world left behind and the world he was striving for.

Benito's feet itched to be moving. His eyes, hungry now, sought all that had shape, all that moved, such as ships racing in the wind, silky sails billowing, or colors dancing against the deep blues of a southern sky.

In the novitiate all was monotony, sameness. Motion existed only in faith, in God's movements in the soul. Each day was a bleak desert of monotony, each day the very same. He jumped out of bed, he prayed, he dined . . . each change of occupation was a sameness because it required no mental adjustment. Each change was accompanied by the same clanging of bells, the same silent, almost imperceptible shifting of persons around him, a land of black ghosts where silence blocked out all laughter and rhythm. Everything was on schedule, a time for everything, humor, appetite, even weariness.

In his crisis de Goes could remember only the world of his own making, the best possible world. Absence made the heart grow fonder because it suppressed the black and brightened the gold. He came to believe that the world he had left was all gold, just as the world he lived in was all black. His novitiate had become tarnished with exposure.

20

The struggle began to tell in terms of health. As the months dragged by, Benito became nervous and thin. He had frequent bouts with headache. He grew irascible with his companions and withdrew more and more into the shell that was natural for him. Pitfalls in the religious life, he was finding out, were far more numerous and more treacherous than any he had known as a soldier. They were more numerous than dangers at sea.

One evening in late spring, 1586, Brother de Goes had his monthly chat with the Master of Novices. Even discussion was routine. As Father Master sat down, he pulled his cassock over his knees and straightened out the wrinkles. His clothes were like his hair, never a thread out of place. He was a tall, willowy Portuguese with wan cheeks and a sharp King Pedro nose. He had been educated for court, and still carried himself more like a grandee than a cleric, though no one would say he was haughty. His movements were natural and elegant, like a duke's among his peers.

"Brother," this ascetic said, and he turned from his thin waxy fingers to de Goes sitting beside him, "I have noticed a long face in the back of the chapel and I'm afraid that it was yours." He waited for Brother to complain of his spiritual aches like a patient to the surgeon.

The "long face" said nothing. Nervous hands plucked at his cincture, and his thoughts were far away.

"Brother, tell me honestly. Have you found peace in the novitiate?"

"I don't know," said de Goes. He looked earnestly into Father Master's eyes. "Father, in a wink I'd give everything—my life even—if I could find peace. You know that."

"Do you know what this peace you seek really is?"

The priest studied the youth's troubled face, the despairing sag in his shoulders.

"Happiness, Father, I want happiness. I cannot find it! Do you see, I can't find it!" He raised his voice as if shouting would convey a message otherwise unintelligible. Father Master said nothing, just watched him, his round dark eyes flashing with infinite understanding.

De Goes raised himself heavily to his feet and paced to the window. Absently searching the skies, he spoke like a man alone, abandoned. "My heart aches for something—I don't know what it is. I've looked for it over half the world. Always it seemed to lie just beyond me, like a rainbow I wanted to touch when I was a boy. Or like the horizon when I sailed into the sun. I thought it would be here. Yes here!" he barked fiercely. "Father, do you hear me, I want music for my soul." He tapped his heart, and his chin stuck out defiantly. "I'll get it where I must."

"You want the moon, so you must have it?" asked Father Master in astonishment. "There is no moon here, nor anything else that a man can grasp by willing it. We are flesh and our novitiate is earth. Here we have hope, not realization.

"Perhaps you had better return to the world. If you're not happy. . . ." He gave a shrug that could have said, "The door is always open."

But Father Master didn't want to say it. If Benito left the novitiate before he had reconciled his hunger with his daily bread, he would become a hopeless misfit. He would be to the end a Gentile seeking manna, forever searching for and fleeing shadows.

"Son, now is the time to speak up. Do you want to leave us?"

"I don't know. This sounds funny to you, I guess."

22

He looked cautiously at Father Master to see if his observations were credible or not. "There's a certain contentment—at night when I crawl into bed and reflect on my day's work. I rather think it pleases God—and it seems to make the fight worthwhile."

Father Master nodded. "Till you are yourself again, why don't you rest in this conviction? God is pleased —why torture yourself?"

"Torture myself?" De Goes always resented references to himself as a cause of his affliction. He was afraid, terribly afraid that he really was the cause, that his struggle, not coming from God, would not even have the saving feature of merit. "Why does God torture me? Is this peace? But a fleeting moment of joy over a day spent in His service?"

The priest said nothing, so Benito calmed down. "Father Master," he begged, "why does God tease me so mercilessly with this frustration—this emptiness?"

"Brother, your peace and happiness will come from a kind of abandonment. When you learn to accept God's will for you, accept yourself, you will be at peace—not one moment before. Let me give you a warning. Your muscles are hard, but your heart is very tender. If you don't face reality—I mean the real reality—you will smash on rocks like your ships, just as surely as you stand on your legs right now."

Father Master shook his head sadly. "You will be the most unhappy of men," he said. "For you it is the top— or the very bottom. And God help you if the bottom!"

After de Goes had closed the stout, chestnut-red door behind him, the novice master stared at it a long time, lost in thought. How many times had he given de Goes the answers, in retreat, in conferences, in discussion, in books. . . . Were words, after all, futile before an emotional blindness? There was no lack of good will, no obstinacy in the novice. Only emptiness, which no man could penetrate.

For several more months Brother de Goes continued to cultivate and water his field of parsnips. And when lilies didn't appear, only parsnips, he determined to find them elsewhere. He packed his clothes and his souvenirs of soldier life, and with his bundle tucked grimly under his arm, he bade goodbye to Father Master and passed into that other world, glittering all gold.

V

A thousand miles south, and more than twice as far east of Italy's ill-shod toe, stretched the Persian Gulf, and on its foaming crest lay the city-island of Ormuz, crossroads of the Old World. The city was five miles off the mainland from which it had been moved two and a half centuries before, to be secure against Tartar raids. It was a city of some forty thousand inhabitants, a sort of Venice of the East where merchants of Arabia, Persia, Armenia, India, China, and of the eastern coast of Africa, met with those of Europe.

The island afforded protection for its inhabitants, but little else. Its soil was so salt-sandy that it could produce nothing, not even decent water for drinking. Everything to sustain life had to be imported, that is everything but heat, for the island was one of the hottest places on earth. It sheltered no birds, no animals. No forests or shrubs or even field grass. It was just a barren, cursed wasteland, floating like a scab on the shining sea.

But Ormuz had "location." Traders, as if they were

defying God's curse, built a great and prosperous city there and so fabulous were its markets and mansions and public buildings that there was a proverb current in the East: "If all the world were a ring, Ormuz would be the gem set into it."

It was this Ormuz of September, 1586, that first received the ex-Jesuit, Benito de Goes. It took the wanderer to its bosom without the slightest acknowledgment, because wanderers in Ormuz were not uncommon.

De Goes in his novitiate days had longed and sighed for something just like Ormuz. A sparkling gem. A city where money flowed like river water and all who cared to remain could have an ocean-cooled mansion and leisure for sporting and rare delicacies to tempt the palate. Couldn't Benito find here the song of life his heart ached to hear? What could be missing save monotony, and of that he had already seen plenty.

He felt as he went up and down the avenues lined with beautiful homes an air of respectability. The material world, he thought, had never reached such heights of grandeur or security. All human ingenuity, all expense, had been called upon to make this a man-made paradise of ease and plenty. The gem, he agreed, in the whole global ring.

He had noticed that Ormuz boasted of its churches. Magnificent temples raised to God, no doubt, by a grateful people who gladly acknowledged the source of all good. The mosque was one of the most beautiful in all the Mohammedan world, its fame surpassing the boundaries of the East. The Christian churches would do honor to any diocese. De Goes was pleased to hear that the bishop, recently deceased, had been pious and zealous and that at least one Jesuit had preached in the episcopal pulpit.

But de Goes was due for a shock. The fact was that Ormuz with all its churches and wealth had gone to seed spiritually, and its shining appearances were nothing more than that, appearances. True, the bishop had been pious and zealous. That's what had carried him off to an early grave, his prayers and tears and heart-break. The native priests were a disgrace to the Christian name. Arabs and Persians had introduced and made common the most detestable kinds of vices, and their Christian followers were as bad as the rest. Murder, for instance, was as common as the dawn, and lawful marriage proportionately rare. As for crooked business, it was a going concern. Merchants made an end of it just for the sheer pleasure of cheating each other. Visitors called them "doctors of usury," and one of de Goes' contemporaries wrote to his friends in Europe that if a theologian came to Ormuz, he would have to start studies all over again. He would have to learn about contracts and exchanges never heard of before.

Such was the real Ormuz, not the streets lined with "respectability" and the ocean-cooled homes with their lovely potted gardens. That it could be for de Goes another novitiate, another school of preparation, only God could say.

The lesson began in a wharf-shop where Benito tarried to watch the ships in the harbor. Always in life he had looked for ships first. But now as he watched—somehow, he couldn't say just why, these ships had lost their charm. They no longer cast a spell over him. To be sure, the beams were right, smooth prows, decks, rigging, white sails flapping on some of them. Yet what were these in view of his loss? When he had traded one world for another, he had reckoned only in terms of gain; now he could realize the cost. What had he given up for this, this harbor at Ormuz? His ideals? That subtle peace he knew so seldom in the novitiate, but only there? Had he cast aside the pearl of great price?

"Throw not pearls before swine!" echoed hollowly in his heart.

Go back to the novitiate! Hurry, perhaps the door has not yet swung shut!

He shook his head sadly, regretting with shame his lack of humility. Too late. Too late to try again, to face the novices who would wonder and ask themselves questions. He must seek elsewhere. Maybe he would find, at length, his place. He was a derelict once more, but even derelicts in their tossings slip into sunny coves and bask till the tides carry them further. Persia! He would try Persia.

And so he sailed to Persia, where he sought all and found nothing. He tried Arabia. Then Baluchistan. Then Ceylon. For two long, weary years he followed the caravan routes up and down the Orient, searching always for something he could not name. But his quest was futile. Material delights, he finally came to understand, turn to dust in the touching. Sense experience was an unwelcome alchemy. It destroyed or altered what anticipation had glorified. For de Goes, as for others, there was only one escape from escape. He determined to take it. It was not a retreat. It was surrender, a surrender with honor and without disgrace because God dictated the terms.

In late 1588, the year of the Spanish Armada's disaster, de Goes retraced his steps to the novitiate at Goa. He presented his request for readmission in the stiff little parlor to a new provincial, Father Peter Martinez. The priest accepted him with tempered expressions of welcome; Benito was remembered and loved. He could move in as soon as he was ready. When the interview was over, Father Martinez pulled out the record book and carefully traced the name:

"Benito de Goes, native of Villa Franca of the Azores, of the Diocese of Portugal, twenty-five years of age, robust in health, readmitted in the year 1588, assigned to household duties."

The novitiate had to begin all over, all but the first six months. It would take Benito two years again, but this time he had a tremendous force to sustain him. He had knowledge of the world that had turned to dust at his touching.

Among the Jesuits this second time, Benito found at last the peace of soul he had been thirsting for, ever since he had sailed from the islands off Portugal. Not in gambling, though he had tried there, not in ship-life, or the gay island-city of Ormuz, not even in a good conscience did Benito find peace. Only in his dedicated work-days, in a final realization that peace is where God puts it, or more exactly, where God puts Benito. Let his parsnips be parsnips. He would accept them and cultivate them as humbly as he knew how.

28

PART 2 • THE CASSOCK

I

Four years after pronouncing his vows Brother De Goes was called from his peaceful routine to adventure. The Provincial had assigned him to accompany Father Jerome Xavier and Father Pinheiro to the court of Akbar, Grand Mogul of the Mogors and Emperor of non-Portuguese India.

Now Father Xavier was a remarkable fellow. To start with, he was a grand nephew of Father Francis Xavier—his grandmother was Father Francis' sister. What was more to his credit, he was considered by all to be a worthy scion of Xavier stock. He was as dauntless as an Albuquerque, and learned and devout. Before his death he had composed a library of Christian writings in the formidable Persian language. He had also been designated coadjutor-archbishop of Crangamore, a lordly but trying office, of which death relieved him.

If Father Jerome was a lion, he would need every sinew of his strength for his mission, because Akbar can be judiciously regarded as one of destiny's greatest rulers. It had often been said that no royal line in the world had presented such a brilliant succession as the Great Moguls. Akbar was the star. In astuteness he outshone those two august contemporaries, Elizabeth and Philip the Second, and he reigned four years longer than either. Despite his several hundred "wives" and rational-istic turn of mind, one is tempted to consider him more Christian than a host of Catholic rulers who came before or after.

Like Philip, but unlike Elizabeth, Akbar was a deeply religious man—in his own rationalistic way. From his youth he had been a devout disciple of Mohammed, and it was even whispered by his more sympathetic admirers that he had tasted the nectar of religious ecstasy.

Of late his credulity in the Prophet had been under-mined. He had called in the mullahs, teachers of the law. The greatest of them had hastened to his side and had unctuously tried to explain away his doubts. In astonish-ment the more intelligent Akbar beat his head and cried, "May God help us! May God help us!"

The overweening mullahs were dismissed, certain Moslem practices banned, and Akbar assumed high-priest prerogatives. He sipped and sipped from the ever-welling fonts of religion in the mystic-fertile Orient.

About this time reports reached him that two Jesuits were at work in the Land of Tea, Bengal, one of his many fabulous provinces. It seems they had created a stir by refusing absolution to Portuguese traders who cheated Akbar of his tax-moneys. The delighted Akbar roared for Jesuits. He must have Jesuits! Now! Im-mediately!

Three letters were dispatched to Goa, one to the Portuguese viceroy, one to Church authorities, one to Jesuit superiors. It is a sad reflection on Elizabeth that she, enlightened Queen of Christian England, hunted out Jesuits for torture and hanging at the very same moment that the infidel Akbar sought them out to grace his court. Could fable be more ironic!

Three separate expeditions left Goa for the Mogul

capital. Benito de Goes belonged to the third. The first was directed by Father Rudolph Acquaviva, only thirty years old, gracious, brilliant, and as ascetical as a desert hermit. He had with him two other Jesuits, one of whom was a converted Moslem.

Acquaviva arrived at Akbar's court at a time when religious debates were the current form of pastime. Not a day passed but that new lawgivers appeared to dispute with the mullahs. Brahmins, Sufis, Shi'-ahs, others with novel and pernicious ideas came out of hiding and advocated their cause with all the fervor of a Moses. Akbar heard them all, though he was accounted a poor listener.

"He asks questions," one of the missionaries complained, "but he starts another subject before an answer is given."

The gentle Acquaviva was soon a royal favorite. He spent most of his time in solitude, living the life of a recluse, giving himself to prayer and the study of Persian. When called upon, he came forth like a David, putting stones to his sling with casual skill. The mullahs soon learned to dread his appearances, but the king, on the other hand, sought him out, sent him tid-bits from the royal table, visited and strolled with him when he could, and made it clear to all that the Padri was in a class by himself.

Encouraged by this familiarity, Father Rudolph spoke very plainly to Akbar. He upbraided him for his many wives, his gladiatorial contests. Akbar took it in the right spirit. He didn't change much, but neither did he murder the bold Padri.

After three years this first Jesuit mission ended in failure. Many friends had been made. Father Rudolph had so endeared himself to the Mogul that he was allowed to depart only on the condition of his promised return. Yet the mission had been a failure. Akbar, the Fathers reported, was not serious. He was attached to a whole host of wives. . . .

Father Rudolph made the weary journey back to Goa, full of thoughts of what might have been. A Christian Akbar. A Christian India to replace the countless apostates in another land. Only what might have been.

In Goa, Acquaviva was given a new assignment and in a few months he was dead. He had been hacked to pieces by the blades of a Christian-hating mob. What might have been . . . a Christian India.

Akbar wept for him. He sent his condolences to Goa in approved Mogor fashion, and added: send more Jesuits. "If they will remain in my court, I shall build them such lodging that they may live in greater honor and favor than any Father who has up to this time been in this country; and when they wish to leave, I shall let them depart with honor. You shall therefore do as I ask of you in this letter. Written at the commencement of the moon of June."

Portuguese officials, for political reasons, urged the Jesuits to comply with Akbar's wishes. The Provincial was willing: two Fathers and a certain Brother Ribeiro answered the summons.

In Lahore they found Akbar less a son of the Prophet Mohammed than before. In fact, he had torn down mosques or used them as elephant stables or storehouses for rice. The Fathers were hopeful. The Emperor, they heard from friends of Father Rudolph, had celebrated the Feast of the Assumption of Mary by publicly paying respect to her picture. He had kissed the image and had placed it on his head, the greatest manifestation of veneration.

34

Soon, all too soon, however, hope vanished. It became plain that Akbar was toying with religion and that nothing could be accomplished. Other works of the Order were pressing, so the Provincial recalled his men to Goa. It was the road of the Anabasis all over again.

If Akbar's pride had suffered from the second Jesuit departure, he didn't openly show it. Instead he meekly dispatched more and more letters to the Jesuits. "Come to instruct me," he begged, "and I will be a willing listener."

An emperor with fifty thousand elephants is not lightly disregarded. He was the door to other missions, or more properly, the key to its golden lock. Father General in Rome said, "Go," and three more Jesuits gathered their scanty belongings. They would try to rescue Akbar from Mammon, but more especially from himself.

I I

In early December Brother de Goes and his companions took to the sea. They left the swamps and monsoons and fevers of Goa Island and turned north to the Mogul capital.

For de Goes it was like homecoming. He had been suckled by the sea. One could almost say that it was his mother. The sea breezes were his bread and cheese. They were tumblers of new wine to his lips. They exhilarated and made him bold and gay. The three-week trip up the coast of India, interminable for the others, was for him all holiday.

At Daman the vessel put in to unload cargo and to take on new burdens, mostly horses and corn and rice.

A few soldiers, too, piled on board, filling the salty air with their laughter. Among them Benito found one who had been stationed a spell at Coleichi. He was enroute to Ormuz, to the Portuguese garrison there.

"What happened to Rodrigo's old woman?" Benito asked him.

Ramon, surnamed Cuiz, was sitting on a deck cannon, his legs dangling heedlessly over the edge of it. "You know that one?" he said without blinking. "She is dead." He blessed himself piously at his own reference to the departed, a sort of reflex ritual like the undertaker's bow.

"She was a good woman," said Benito, anxious to say something proper.

"Yes, good but old. Very old," said Ramon, and he spat out his displeasure. "Now Marcelina—but of course you couldn't have met Marcelina!"

"Of course not," said Benito blushing a little. He remembered her well—Marcelina who loved too freely. "But there was João, a young fellow, darling of the village." He wondered if Ramon had noticed how abruptly he had changed the subject.

"That one Ho ho!" Ramon recalled something hilariously funny about João. He slapped Benito on the shoulder with reckless familiarity. "The Padri—you should have seen the Padri!"

"Yes?" said Benito.

"He sent João to St. Paul's College in Goa—to be a priest if you please. In a few months João came back—with a wife! You should have seen that Padri!"

It was now ten years since he saw that Padri.

After a day or two of delay in Daman, the vessel cleared port and sought the open sea again to gain Cambay before the favorable winds were gone. No storms impeded their progress. The rainy season had just

36

passed and with it the clouds of trade. Sunshine brought a new tone of optimism that bade fair for merchants and shippers.

In another week the sturdy little tub crossed the shallow bar at the entrance to Cambay Bay and slipped through scores of Portuguese frigates rocking to and fro with the gentle swells. Without effort or fuss it dropped its anchor and settled down to await customs inspection. Beyond the fringe of the harbor gleamed the tiled roofs of a not-very-large city, but, judging from appearances, a wealthy one. Also a fortified one, for Portuguese guns covered the waters from all angles with a business-like readiness.

The visitors had to wait because in the East no one hurried, except sailors before a brisk breeze, or nervous Jesuits, and the custom inspectors were neither. In the interim a fleet of small boats surrounded their ship and business was taken up in earnest. The occupants of these boats were called brokers and they made their living by conducting sales for merchants who arrived from other lands. They were very powerful and wealthy as well, each one having fifteen or twenty servants to assist him in his business. Though they could not conclude their contracts till the merchants' goods had passed inspection, they usually hurried out to incoming ships to solicit clients. Once a contract was made between merchant and broker, the former had nothing more to do in Cambay until the latter gave him his money for the sale, or other goods to take to another port.

While the brokers shouted back and forth, Akbar's three missionaries put on their Sunday best and prepared to storm Cambay. By imperial order, they were exempt from customs-inspection, and Father Jerome was determined to press the point as soon as inspectors appeared to do their duty.

"What can they know about Christian baggage?" he snorted. "Besides, we must hurry. . . ."

Within several hours, Father Jerome had his way and the three Jesuits were permitted to go ashore.

Cambay had seen many strange sights since its last king was killed in siege and since Akbar, the Grand Mogul, had added it to his realm in 1572. But none was more astonishing than the invasion of three Jesuits in that week before Christmas, 1594. The harbor buzzed with commerce until their arrival. Then, as the three clean-shaved teachers of the law, clad in flowing black robes, with heads stuck in wide hats as black and shiny as ravens, gravely clambered to the dock, a new climax was reached and all business momentarily ceased. Cambayans literally stopped in their tracks to gape at this new wonder. Shop-keepers poked their heads out. Incredibly small men dropped incredibly large burdens. Boys, fishermen, sailors, idlers—all saw the strange trio and gaped at them in wonder.

Unmindful of Cambay's consternation, the invaders proceeded slowly up the quay to port authorities and serenely spread out credentials for any and all inspection. When the officials regained their breath and examined the credentials, their wonder turned to obeisance. These freaks were under the special patronage of Akbar himself! Like magic an Armenian servant appeared to provide for their immediate needs.

He was a dark, inscrutable fellow with teeth like a snow ridge sparkling and bright in the dusk of his cheeks. All he lacked was a lamp to be Aladdin, and even without it, he mysteriously assured his charges that he could produce anything. He would conjure up rooms,

38

house-servants, food, pack-animals—even Christians. And he did.

In Cambay many houses, partly furnished, were kept open for visiting merchants. The Jesuits were directed to one of these. They found it a most suitable arrangement, a house with a courtyard, sleeping quarters, and one large room besides. Within a few hours Brother de Goes had converted the latter into a chapel. He decorated it so lavishly with tapestries and flowers that before he was finished pagan visitors flocked to examine it. Droves of them came. With the unrestrained curiosity common to an Eastern people, they stood about and simply gawked at the exhibition (including Benito) till they were pushed out of the way by others who came to do likewise.

Many of them were women, bold creatures who "modestly" declined to show their faces. They peered brazenly over their veils and rattled countless bracelets made of elephants' teeth on their arms, attachments so dear to them that they'd rather be without food than their bracelets.

There were more than a few Portuguese families in the city, most of them traders who had been caught like pawns in the money-game of a fading era. These joyfully trooped to the Fathers and attended the Masses and innumerable sermons.

One of their number had turned yogi, "the devil holding him ensnared in many great and grievous sins," according to one account. The yogi joined his compatriots in a solemn renunciation of Satan and all his pomps and devoutly received Holy Communion. What was more difficult in a practical way, he cleared his roomy harem and took back his one legitimate wife.

While these edifying festivities were taking place, the

39

second son of the Great Mogul, Sultan Murad by name, arrived in the neighborhood. He was making war for his father and had a vast army encamped outside the city. Hearing of the Jesuits' presence, he sent a note to them. Would the exalted Fathers meet him in a castle within the city? Could they come at once?

Yes, the Fathers could come. To be sure, it was quite late, and Christmas Eve at that, but anxious to pay their respects they hastened to the castle. The Prince received them with great kindness and honor. He was a bit formal, the Fathers said afterwards, but obviously had good intentions.

To their immense relief the visitors were soon dismissed. The Prince had achieved his purpose in town, the collection of two hundred thousand crowns of gold in coins and ingots, and he wished to return to camp. The next day, with his warriors, he rattled off to Surrate a few miles south. Here he set up another camp and looked about him for means of amusing himself.

He wasn't an efficient man, this Sultan Murad. In fact, he spent much of his time in running hither and thither and in love-making, a circumstance which scandalized the Fathers when they heard it, for they had been led to expect great things from him. When he was but a lad of thirteen, Father Acquaviva had been his tutor. "We hope," wrote the teacher in 1582, "to see some fruit from the Emperor's second son, Pahari, a boy of thirteen years of age, who is learning the Portuguese language, and therewith the things relating to our faith, and who shows himself well disposed thereto, and who is of great natural genius and has good inclination. . . ."

But now the fruit was evidently bitter, and the Fathers could see worse to come.

A week after Christmas, the bored-with-routine Prince

ordered another visit from the Jesuits. "Bring them here," he commanded the royal messenger service.

The black-robes were summarily shaken off their mats at three in the morning. "But the Feast of the Circumcision!" gasped Father Pinheiro.

No matter. They had to go. Father Jerome celebrated Mass. All three bustled off in the darkness. Sultan Murad's tent was reached at the hour army captains and lesser lords assembled to pay their homage to sovereignty. They stood like statues, eyes glued to the Prince, as the Jesuits approached the purple pavilion.

The Prince was most affable this morning. No, nothing important. He wanted to chat.

"Is there ice and snow in Portugal?" he asked.

"Oh, my lord, yes." Father Jerome sighed and rolled his eyes with exasperation. He looked toward Benito and his eyes said, "Five hours on horseback for this!"

Aloud he said, "Lots of snow, especially in the hills and mountains. But only during winter months."

"Well," exclaimed the Prince, turning to his captains. "So they have these things in Portugal too. Do they have bears?"

"Oh yes, my Lord."

"Ah, they have bears," to his captains. "Do they have rabbits?"

"Yes, my Lord, many rabbits."

"What about birds of the chase, falcons and hawks, do they have these?"

"Yes, my Lord. The falcons are trained by experts. The King and his nobles keep hundreds of them." Father Jerome began to hope that the Prince's animal repertoire was as limited as his taste for study.

Perhaps the Prince sensed Xavier's dislike for the conversation about bears and rabbits. He changed the subject to more serious topics, like Portugal's roads and what was done to punish robbers. He constantly repeated Xavier's comments to the courtiers, as if these worthies were a thousand miles hence while Xavier spoke. They grimaced and bowed in acknowledgement. They were honored to be included in the distinguished discussion and they placed their hands on the ground, palms down, then on their heads to say so.

"Ah, they have many things in Portugal," said the Prince, in the manner of saying the last word. He rose from his pillows. "Come with me, my exalted Fathers." He strolled with them out of the gathering and ascended a mound of earth.

"I know you do not accept gifts. But you are poor men. You will need money on your journey. I have instructed my attendants to give your guide these fifteen hundred *manudes*." He patted a bag of coins that had been brought to him.

"I want you to accept this, for I give it as an alms. Do you have passports?"

Xavier said yes, thank you, the passports were made out for the kingdom of Schind.

"Hmmm." Prince Murad paused to think whether this would do or not. He was evidently satisfied, for he nodded, then stepped from the earth-mound onto the back of a small elephant. From this to a larger one, and with a bob of the head he was away.

Before leaving the camp the Jesuits were shown what had been gathered to intimidate the Deccans, arch-foes of Akbar and present objectives of Prince Murad's campaign. Twenty-five thousand horsemen, four hundred elephants, seven hundred camels, forty or fifty dromedaries, four thousand bullocks, nineteen pieces of cannon, and some smaller guns. Nevertheless, the priests agreed with Brother Benito that the Prince had little hope of success. It was all too evident that he was unduly influenced by a reckless, corrupted group around him, a crowd of unprincipled youths who paid little heed to their elders. They were bent on one course, to get all they could out of the liberal, good-natured Prince before his star had set.

Between Cambay and Lahore, Akbar's capital, lay a vast, bleak desert. Sand, weeks of sand stretched before the wayfarer like some geographical sin. Often windstorms whirled up in these dismal wastes and travellers lost their way and were buried in the sands forever. They were victim-tributes demanded by the desert that others might trespass.

Robber bands infested the region. Some of these bands were five hundred strong, and employed all the latest devices of violence, war elephants, and muskets seized from the weak. To protect themselves against these grim marauders, travellers formed caravans. Prospective caravaneers had to search out others with similar intentions and haggle over times and departures and equipment and a thousand other trifles. Prospects met in bazaars over coffee or candies. After much patience, tact, and talk a plot gradually evolved, a plan which might require many more days for ripening.

After a seemingly endless wait in the City of Pillars, Brother de Goes and the Fathers at last found a caravan destined for Lahore. When it gathered, it was a nondescript outfit, four hundred camels, a hundred carts and horses, and a host of poor folk who trusted to foot. The Jesuits had been given three carts and six bullocks by the Sultan Murad. With these they were able to help their less fortunate brethren, to relieve for just a wee moment part of the burden India's poor must bear.

43

In February, the caravan finally got started. The cara-vaneers had chosen one of their members to be captain and all scrupulously obeyed him lest they be banished for mutiny. Banishment was a matter of almost certain death. According to custom, drums served as stop-and-go signals, as tocsins and curfews. When the drums rattled in the early dawn, the Jesuits lowered and folded their tents. Drums rattled again. Dum-dee-dum-dum! They loaded their carts. Dum-dee-dum-dum! The caravan began its tedious crawl. During these operations the captain in charge was everywhere, shouting, waving his sword, cursing the tardy, anything and everything to get the wagons rolling and keep them that way. And as they moved along, he passed from the front to the rear lines, or *vice versa*, forty times a day, apparently never satisfied with progress or the condition of the trail. His was a heavy responsibility, because one day's delay might mean disaster.

Often the procession was forced by brigands or water shortage to continue through the night. On such occasions the drummers led the way and filled the desert emptiness with their percussions. It was not as ingenious as the Hebrews' Pillar of Fire, but as a device it served to hold the caravan together and that, in the circumstances, was magic enough.

Progress was desperately slow because the loaded camels moved heavily. Their innards were supplied with almost bottomless water reservoirs, but they were geared down to a snail's pace and no amount of tinkering, Benito discovered, could alter their pace.

By mid-March, the voyagers reached an imposing walled city hard by a river's edge. It was Ahmadabad, capital of its province and hub of a far-flung trade. The Jesuits, moved more by curiosity than zeal, took in the

44

sites, and soon found plenty to write home about. Not the least was a yogi, a renowned, honest-to-goodness yogi.

Like others of his trade, he was adept at all manner of tricks; and so zealous was he that he practised more terrifying austerities than all other yogis of the kingdom. Precisely for this he was esteemed as a great saint and crowds flocked to see him.

The "saint" was, however, especially conceited. He was most contemptuous of the sinners who gathered about him to marvel at his bony anatomy or to kiss the soles of his feet, an homage carefully provided for by the proper posture. Holy, holy yogi! The man was little more than a mummy in his scanty windings, with his massive head and bulbous, watery eyes, his shaggy chin, prominent ribs, and leg joints swollen with the Hard Life, his feet just so, a holy spectacle resplendent on mats of leopard skin. It was a faultless performance, too, at least until Sultan Murad caught up with it.

This happened while the Jesuits were in the city. Their friend, the Prince, was in the neighborhood, and hearing of the yogi's fame, he sent for him.

"Tell the Prince," sneered the yogi to the official embassy, "if he wants to see me, he can come here, for my holiness well merits it."

Now as anyone could imagine, the Prince was little taken in by yogis in general and by Ahmadabad's yogi in particular. Hence he lost no time in ordering a sound thrashing for the scoundrel and, for good measure, banishment from the province. That was one way of handling an arrogant "saint," but not an effective one. It but added martyrdom to his spiritual conquests.

There was another item of great interest in Ahmadabad, a shrine which housed the bones of a great teacher. The Jesuits visited the place, not to be freed from their sins as the Mohammedans believed, but to examine a building which was very famous throughout the East. It had been built by a grateful King who had studied under the deceased. It was constructed entirely of highly polished marble, of beautiful tint and markings, and had several inner courts, in one of which Father Pinheiro counted four hundred and fifty pillars, each thirty feet high, with bases and capitals in best Corinthian. The Jesuits were so impressed that they immediately disassociated its beauty from the "barbarous land about" and declared it "free of all barbarism."

From Ahmadabad, five days of caravaneering over sixty miles brought the Jesuits to Pantana, where they tarried long enough to celebrate Easter.

Some Christians, who had of late joined the caravan, confessed to the Fathers and shared their Paschal observances. Others, who were Armenians, pretended to be shocked at these liturgical feastings. They said the Fathers had not calculated the Lenten time correctly, and that it was not Easter yet, but rather the season of penance. Easter would come, to be sure, after five more weeks.

Brother Benito quietly joined in the dispute. In fact, he took it over and won a reluctantly conceded victory. Didn't these Armenians know that the Pope had changed the calendar? Yes, they knew, but they didn't observe the new calendar. Well, Portugal did. Were they not under the ecclesiastical jurisdiction of Portugal? Let the Armenians be sensible and follow the advice of these two Fathers of our holy company.

All finally yielded to this persuasion. That is, all but one who was more obstinate than scrupulous. He professed to be a doctor, a learned one he would have them

46

know, and he made his stand clear to all. The glorious Feast of the Resurrection he celebrated alone on the Sunday before Ascension Thursday.

As the caravan approached the journey's end, it passed through countless villages and cities which lay mostly in ruins. The Jesuits were particularly heartened by the remnants of mosques on all sides. "They are not rebuilt," said Father Jerome with the deepest satisfaction. Surely the Mogors would very soon become Christians!

III

"My possessions are yours," Akbar was saying as he embraced Father Jerome Xavier. "I hope your journey has been pleasant . . . take rest and food. . . ."

He passed from one Jesuit to another like an anxious dowager welcoming her guests. In like fashion his son, the Prince Salim, went through the ceremony, with less warmth perhaps, but with impeccable ease.

"Your Majesty, we have been well attended. These captains graciously met us at the city gate and have escorted us here. I trust Your Majesty will reward them?"

"Ah yes. Yes, yes. It gives me great pleasure to see the exalted and holy Fathers. I have waited long—so long." He brightened a little. "But now you are here, my eternal thanks to the Christian authorities."

Akbar's whole bearing manifested his concern for propriety. His was an easy dignity. He was part of the surroundings, like the canopy over his head.

Brother Benito had suffered the welcoming ceremonies with as much heart as any shy and unassuming person might. He withdrew now to the shadows, a vantage

47

point from which he could examine the central figure in the plush throne room. The renowned Akbar was hardly the despotic type, he decided. Neither a Goliath nor a diminutive like David. His most notable feature was his Oriental swarthiness, a Tartar characteristic that suggested his lineal descent from Tamerlane. His eyes confirmed this ancestry, and Benito could see shining in them the specter of the "Scourge of God," a barbarian. Despite this unwelcome relationship, Akbar was groomed with discriminating taste. His garments gleamed with the gold from which they were spun. Gems on the wrist and about the neck were not ostentatious, just touches of vanity that an Occidental usually expected to find among women.

Akbar, squatting cross-legged on a throne of velvet and gold, now inquired most diligently about the latest developments in Portuguese India. He admired very much (so he said) the valor and skill of the Portuguese. Their cannon foundry at Chaul was highly respected—and envied—by all the princes of India. Now there was an important development, cannons. . . .

While the discussion progressed, Benito watched the monarch very closely. He noted the head cocked lightly to one side, an affectation associated, in Benito's mind, with the self-conscious ascetic. Could it mean that he was self-conscious at all times, or just in the presence of persons he respected? Or feared?

As the royal head turned now to this one, now to another, Benito couldn't fail to observe its indefinable mark of mystery, the enigmatic expression, a mask which concealed, perhaps, the profound workings within. For all that, there was not a great deal more to indicate profoundness. A smooth chin, but an upper-lip marked with a small, neatly trimmed moustache. On the left side of the nose, for all to see, shone a pea-sized mole, very dear to its bearer, Benito was to learn, for those skilled in physiognomy considered the wart "a sign of great prosperity and exceeding good fortune."

His Majesty had a reputation for stinginess, and Benito searched carefully for indications of it. Perhaps, he thought jocosely, the king had to be stingy. A man with one wife should understand. Gowns and bonnets for several hundred women would keep a Midas bankrupt! Benito chuckled to himself over his own modest joke, thinking whether Father Emmanuel or Father Jerome knew enough about women to appreciate it.

Certainly the old Tartar was munificent with the Jesuits. He provided a large, quiet house near the river far removed from the turmoil of the market. He sent over servants and guards, who were on duty day and night, and a thousand other little attentions, like candles for the altar and special dishes from his own kitchen. He received them at court at all times with a kindly spirit, and whenever he met one of them he bowed his head in reverence. Nothing that could make the Jesuits feel welcome was omitted.

The day following their arrival at Lahore, that is, on the sixth of May, the Jesuits were drawn again into the royal radiance. Akbar had paintings to show them, one of Christ and one of the Virgin, Father Rudolph's first gifts nearly ten years before. Seeing the sacred images, the visitors fell to their knees to manifest devotion and respect to the Saviour and His Mother. Akbar's eight-year-old grandson aped this behaviour, folding his hands after the fashion of the Fathers. He looked like a plump little cherub out of Raphael, and old Grandpa was delighted.

"Look at your son!" he piped to Prince Salim.

Of course, this pleased all concerned, all save the confirmed Moslems at court, who could see nothing but doom in the arrival of the priests.

"Come see the books Father Rudolph has presented me." Akbar proudly displayed the collection. He handed them one by one to Father Jerome. Some were upside down, for Akbar despite his great learning could neither read nor write.

"*Summary of Theology by St. Thomas,*" read Father Pinheiro, and Akbar nodded knowingly. He shifted the paintings he still carried to the other arm.

De Goes, at this point, offered to carry the pictures for him.

"No, no," said Akbar. He was so attached to the things that he fondled them constantly. He could never be persuaded to put them aside till his arms ached with the bulk of them.

"*Commentary of Cajetan,*" said Father Jerome. "*History of the Popes, Chronicle of St. Francis, Spiritual Exercises of Father Ignatius*—even a Latin Grammar. Why, these books are priceless!*"

"Oh yes," Akbar agreed most eagerly. He insisted that the Fathers take them to their house. It was only a loan, His Majesty explained, and the Fathers laughingly approved.

Prince Salim inquired about other paintings. Had the guides of the Fathers brought other works from Goa? No! Indeed this was a keen disappointment. He treasured pictures "of our Lady." "The Madonna," he added, with touching ingenuousness. He was most interested in securing others at any cost.

The Fathers, attributing his concern for Madonnas to piety, looked at one another as if to remark, "Well,

50

what do you say—he'll make a fine convert." Little did they know of his passion for paintings.

"My Lord," said Father Jerome, "we have brought with us a man of oil and brushes. He is at your service."

The Prince beamed with gratitude. Had he been younger, he would have whooped at the prospect, but instead he gave Xavier a quick bow and hurried out with his newly acquired treasure. A Portuguese artist with whom he couldn't speak a word!

In the ensuing weeks Father Jerome was determined to learn all he could about the man they had come a thousand miles to win, and he didn't have to look far for information. The royal person was common property, along the gossip-routes of India. Indeed, he was too common, a never-ending subject of opinion or oath, of concern, or scorn, or envy, or a hundred other emotions that rule mankind. All Xavier had to do was keep his ears and eyes open and his man emerged as he was, the most consequential figure in all of contemporary Asia.

"Slayer of Hostile Kings" he called himself. He made much of this, but in practice was too soft-hearted to slay anyone, unless, of course, rage or a sense of frustration had seized him. He ordered killing only when absolutely forced to, and even then, instructed the executioners to await a third command before putting it into effect. He was always overjoyed to find any excuse for pardon, and a pardon meant that the incident was entirely forgotten.

In his personal tastes, Akbar was considered abstemious. He slept but three hours out of twenty-four. Throughout the remaining wee hours of night his mail was read to him, reams of monthly reports from distant captains. About food he was most indifferent. He ate but once a day and that at irregular times. He simply called for his meal. Within the hour it was ready for him, usually rice with milk, and lastly candies for a tenderly cherished sweet tooth. For the rest of his courtiers he kept elaborate kitchens with cooks of all nations. Every conceivable delicacy appeared on the royal table.

More edifying than all this were tales of his kindness to the poor. If he acted cold and aloof toward the nobles, he never did so toward the lowly. He was always accessible to them. Their gifts he accepted with all graciousness, pressing them to his breast to manifest his gratitude. He often worked with the poor. He sheared his smelly camels. He hewed stone. He cut wood. He made his own shoes, from his own designing. In the basement of his palace he had an iron works, where he labored at casting cannons with his iron-smiths and joked like other ordinary mortals.

It was all bewildering to de Goes, whose knowledge of kings was limited to the rather pompous despots of the Western world or to the petty of the Eastern. Akbar had so much of the saint about him, virtues rarely found in the hearts of the mighty. How close he was to St. Louis, greatest of the kings of France!

And yet, how far! Man is friend of God, or enemy. There is no in-between status. Could Akbar yield a little—so very little—his place as an intimate of God would be assured. The question of the moment was this: would he yield that very little? The Jesuits would have to wait for the answer.

As for himself, Brother Benito didn't favor court life. He attended when he was called, and this was often, for Akbar had taken a fancy to him. He was asked to sit on the gold and velvet cushions with His Majesty, a triumph reserved to the ruler and his sons. With great simplicity, Benito settled back into the pillows and beamed upon the crowned kings standing below him. What a life! Picture Spain's Philip with a Jesuit on his lap!

From his throne Benito was called upon to offer advice on affairs of state. Advice for the great Akbar! Well, he gave it with frankness and firmness. No flattery, no double talk here, and Akbar was quick to appreciate it.

Did the Brother know about Bengal? Bengal was a rich province—tea, that was the source of its wealth. It had Imperial posts where soldiers were quartered. Did the Brother approve of soldiering and professional officers whose business it was to use force when necessary? What means did Christian kings use for paying their armies of soldiers? Did the Christian law condemn princes who took others as prisoners and forced them to make submission?

Court life was a succession of pageants, for every day princes appeared to make their submission. They crawled up to the throne and groveled like simpering dogs, all to keep a crown on their silly heads. What poppycock! How many would grovel thus to attain an eternal crown? Not many, Benito reckoned.

Akbar, he noticed, was quite liberal in treating with subject kings, even allowing them to keep their crowns in court, their shiny baubles. At times as many as twenty kings stood in attendance, each balancing the center of his universe on a precarious head and bowing and smiling on all that was done. Akbar was the greatest of mortals, favored son of heaven, most illustrious of warriors (how true!). And so on, and so on. Behind their gracious masks they measured the "tyrant's" years and plotted vengeance, which they knew would never be realized. The old fox was too sly. And they, petty souls, had hearts like chickens.

On one occasion de Goes saw a conquered king make his first obeisance. This wretched rascal, when he entered the hall and was yet a long way off, was forced to bow down till his head touched the ground. Then advancing little by little, he repeated the performance till he was near the throne. Guards searched him for concealed weapons. None were discovered; so he was allowed to approach and kiss the Emperor's feet. The latter made no other sign of his good will than that of placing his hand on the vassal's neck.

After paying his homage, the subject king stood up and withdrew to a place assigned him while attendants brought in his gifts. Swords and sheaths of ruby-studded gold, golden vessels, four carpets of fabulous value. Another attendant announced gifts fetched to Akbar's stables, a splendidly caparisoned horse with harness crusted with precious stones and gold, one hundred and fifty other horses, and fifty camels trimmed in green and crimson velvet.

At the same time presents arrived from the eldest Mogul son, Sultan Murad. Fifty elephants, two chariots, one of gold and one of silver, and lastly a tray of mother-of-pearl knick-knacks for the Emperor's collection.

Akbar really did bathe in silver and gold!

Whatever might be said of the official attitude toward the Jesuits in Lahore, there was certainly no doubt about popular opinion. Lahore's populace had little respect for these foreign "liverless pigs and dogs."

As Brother Benito went about the streets helping beggars or cripples, he was often the butt of insults and brickbats. It didn't bother him much. It simply reminded him of St. Francis, who serenely hopped along while the urchins of Assisi hurled choice epithets about his ears. Benito's heart ached for the little tots who knew no better. There was no greater hardship for him in exile than the spectacle of countless souls he met who knew not Jesus Christ, the one true God.

"Their false prophet," he growled, "that is all I hear, the unholy name of their false prophet."

On all sides, Lahore's rejection was amply evident. "Black devils," the people hissed when they passed. "*Siah Posh*" was another term used, but this implied greater respect, or rather, less disrespect. It meant "those dressed in black." The miserable "*Siah Posh*" were Portuguese, the hated race in the Indies. What was worse, they were responsible for the Emperor's apostasy and religious scruples.

There was the rub. What were the Emperor's religious scruples? The Fathers talked and talked. It was always the same conclusion—Akbar's conversion was as remote as ever. He pretended to have a dogmatic doubt about the Trinity (he was scandalized at mystery), but his reasons for procrastination were quite otherwise. On the one hand, he was attached to countless wives. On the other, he had an overpowering ambition to be considered a spiritual prophet or a demi-god. What did Mohammed have that he did not! And Mohammed held the fierce allegiance of millions!

He liked to think of himself as the founder of a sect. Abkar had followers, the Jesuits were told, either for bribery or to flatter him. They came to him for miracles and he grandiosely presented them with the water he had bathed his feet in, that they might heal their sick with it. Young women paid vows to him for the safe delivery of their children; and when offspring arrived, they hastened to his feet to bring alms, trifles that he valued more than his crown.

Into his "faith," the broad-minded founder dashed a generous portion of Catholicism. One often saw him reverencing portraits of Christ and His Mother. Around his neck he carried a reliquary with a carving of Our Lady on one side and an *Agnus Dei* on the other.

Once he popped in on the Jesuit community as they were about to begin their daily "Litanies." Akbar remained on his knees with hands clasped until they finished. Afterwards he wandered about the chapel prying into this and that. He was especially fascinated by the pictures on the walls and he stood before each long and attentively.

The Fathers adroitly used this incident to throw him a hint. How nice His Majesty's copy of St. Luke's Madonna would look just here! To be sure, only for the Feast of the Assumption. Akbar swallowed the bait. He sent St. Luke over for the occasion and included hangings of silk and gold that they might keep for the chapel.

On another occasion, the King came to Mass. He was bitterly disappointed that Father Jerome hadn't shared the Chalice with him. "You ate and drank and didn't offer me anything," he complained afterwards.

Catholic litanies of the saints were very well. Mass was very well. But the moral law was too firm and unyielding. The great monarch of England had been refused the liberty of a *second* wife? Incredible. And he had gone into schism. It was folly to trade one's peace of soul for another wife. Ah, how well Akbar knew that lesson!

Oh yes, the Grand Mogul was greatly in favor of others' entering the Catholic Church. He encouraged it among his courtiers, made merry on their baptismal days, and showered them with attentions. He was like the enthusiastic swimmer who cautiously hugged the brink while urging others to make the icy plunge. A brisk dip was good for all but himself.

Father Emmanuel Pinheiro wanted a showdown. Either—or. He was more outspoken than Xavier, sometimes daringly waggish with the king. The latter suffered it goodnaturedly because Pinheiro was a favorite of his. He had entirely adopted the ways of the Mogors—all but the morals. For this he was jokingly nicknamed "The Mogul" by his Jesuit confreres, and even those abroad addressed him by that title. Father Emmanuel didn't mind; in fact, he rather liked it.

Father Jerome, on the other hand, favored caution. "The time will come," he said, and he patiently shouldered his cross of waiting. Time did improve Akbar's opportunities for reflections on the vanity of his world, for Providence rapped his knuckles thrice within the next few months.

I V

Brother de Goes shifted uneasily on Akbar's pillows and prepared himself for a long royal harangue. He had attended court often lately, too often. Ever since news had come from Sultan Murad, Akbar had become despondent over the Deccan war. He had insisted on Benito's companionship.

"Brother is good medicine for the devil and the dumps," he told Xavier, using an expression he had borrowed from Father Pinheiro. He hadn't explored to the full its meaning, but he liked it.

"Brother de Goes," Akbar had said repeatedly during those dark days, "I need some of your peace and serenity."

"Your Majesty," Benito would reply, "you know whence my peace comes. Why don't you draw near and take some for yourself?"

"Yes, yes." Akbar always answered in that tone mildly suggestive of impatience. "Brother de Goes . . ." Akbar started to speak when he spotted a disturbance at the entrance to his chamber. "What can this fuss be?" he said petulantly.

"Not another report of a lost war and twelve captains dead!" Abdullah Mirza made this remark pointedly. He had never favored the Mogul son's generalship.

The reference was painful to Akbar, but he suffered the Abdullah's barb in silence and feigned great interest in the commotion at the door.

Out of the swirl wiggled a road-weary courier, who rushed through the ceremonial bows and approached the king, breathing heavily.

"Your Majesty." He puffed some more, then blurted it out. "Sultan Murad is dead!"

Akbar stared incredulously. "Dead?" he gasped. As the truth seeped in, his eyes watered and he looked from one to another for confirmation of this intelligence. No face could deny it nor tongue tell him he was dreaming.

"Did he . . ." Akbar turned to the courier, but he spoke to no one in particular. He was a man in a world apart, very small and all alone. "Did he die honorably?" he asked in a dull monotone.

"In battle, Your Majesty."

Well put. The courier could have said a lot more. He could have said what others were saying, that the favorite son had died from drink. Thirty years old and a dead drunkard. The details were not pleasant.

But no one pressed the point. The son had died in battle—honorably.

With careful haste court attendants offered their expressions of sympathy, then took a thief-like departure. Only Benito remained to comfort the king, who was, above all, a father, numb with grief and still uncomprehending the moment's significance. Benito was "good medicine for the devil and the dumps."

By Holy Week Akbar had recovered somewhat from fate's latest blow. He had even come to take enough interest in his affairs to officiate at sun-worship and to act as chairman at a sun-sectarian convention. He had gathered the several delegates in a breezy pavilion adjoining the palace, a lovely place overlooking pools with water lilies and lotus flowers which had been brought hence from China. The convention had just about come to a decision on the functions to be observed for their New Year. All were yessing the chairman (with flawless judgment and vigor) when the chairman suddenly shouted, "Look!"

One of the awnings near by had burst into flames. The most sacred worthies were so astonished that no one made a move till it was too late. The flames leaped from tent to tent along the terrace.

"Fire! Fire!" yelled Akbar, hoarse with fear lest his world be lost.

Soon the palace itself and the whole estate was a roaring inferno.

Ancestral treasures, golden thrones, silks and cloths-of-gold, gem-crusted scimitars and votive trifles, all had to be abandoned to the hungry flames which knew no satisfaction. The throne rooms blazed, the royal library, the harem. Women shrieked and scurried about like denizens of a doomed ant-hill. Rivulets of melted gold and silver oozed like heavy water down garden paths. And for three days Akbar wept while his Rome burned.

Life's nectar had turned to vinegar and gall. Akbar's trinkets were gone, his priceless trinkets. His wooden-canvas paradise was a shambles, black, charred like an ugly hell. He could scarcely bear the sight of it, yet its very ugliness and emptiness fascinated him. It stirred the melancholy within him, but its soothing was only skin-deep. Akbar was pierced down deep in the heart, where no skin-balm could ease the pain.

De Goes was at his side to urge a lesson, but in his grief Akbar didn't grasp it. God whispers in prosperity, said Benito. He shouts in pain. Akbar was deaf in either case and the lesson was lost, like the armies and the son and all the treasures.

After melancholy and self-pity had failed, physicians prescribed other remedies for Akbar. The patient, they agreed, must take himself elsewhere, to scenes better calculated to raise his despairing spirits. Camels waddled and carts rolled. The king climbed his elephant and Father Jerome and Brother Benito, by royal command, climbed theirs. They were off to the Province of Kashmir for a holiday.

Lovely Kashmir was India's Switzerland. It wasn't so much an isolated mountain fastness as a playground, a sort of continental park where the rich could summer in mile-high air-conditioned comfort. Like Switzerland it offered a folder of attractions: mountain climbing, fishing, sailboating, hunting, or just plain rusticating. For the pious there were shrines and for the shopper, markets loaded down with produce of every kind: souvenirs or home furnishings or clothes. Especially clothes, like the fine, smooth shawls and the hooded cloaks called "scials," for which Kashmir was famous.

To arrive at his resort the Kashmir vacationist had to suffer what was euphemistically called "a mountain road." The "road" was a rocky trail very much like a staircase up mountains piled one on the other, through valleys where ice was like marble and where the sun never penetrated, in and out of freezing cold streams and lion-skulking jungles, and finally down into a vast, bowl-shaped valley. The descent was shared with rivers which dropped from glaciers somewhere near the sky. It was stony and steep and pack animals often broke their necks.

But it was worth it. The lush Kashmir Valley was worth any man's effort to capture it, like a fairy castle way up in the clouds. Trees covered it like a sacred grove. There were orchards of pear, apple, peach, plum, apricot, walnut, almond. There were grape vineyards, too, and the whole pattern was carefully tied in with endless beds of roses and iris and daisies.

Srinagar (called "Kashmir," too, by the natives), capital of this mountain empire, lay in the Valley's midriff. It was a wool market, a shop where wool of the tus, shawl-goat of Tibet, was weaved into fine fabrics and rugs by Kashmir's quick, cunning fingers. Its folk were simple and friendly, like the Swiss. All day long they would patiently display their wares to tourists, and often enough they sold nothing. But they never complained. They worshiped the god of Hinduism and hated no man. Ordinarily food was plentiful and cheap and they were happy.

Near Srinagar, Akbar had a villa. It sprawled across an artificial island in the midst of a deep, sweet-watered lake. Ducks swept down from Tibetan highlands just to be the privileged targets of His Majesty's musket-shot and arrows. The king dearly loved duck-hunting.

It was to this villa that Akbar brought his household in the late spring of 1597. Servants transported a thousand barge-loads of "conveniences" out to the island and Akbar moved in with noisy relief. This was the life! Why did men pursue so relentlessly the comforts of city-living?

Xavier and de Goes settled down with him. They enjoyed their new surroundings, but they had not forgotten what business they had come to promote, particularly now that Akbar had leisure to discuss affairs of the soul. Xavier had it all planned. He would remind the king of God's blessings showered so lavishly on his house, of God's punishments for those who despise His law. Surely after the chastisements he had just received, he would abandon his wickedness and embrace the holy law. So thought Xavier.

But little came of it. Shortly after their arrival in Kashmir, both Xavier and de Goes were stricken "with a fever," that ever-recurring plague of Europeans in Asia. For several weeks both kept to their mats while the king busied himself with attentions. He sent his own physicians to prescribe herbs and roots for them, and on occasion he even visited them in person, a phenomenon so rare that it had never been heard of before.

When the Jesuits recovered, the king took sick. For the rest of the summer he needed his own physicians and purges and blood-lettings. He was obviously in no mood for encouragement to bend his proud neck and to dismiss a whole army of wives, all save one; so Xavier was forced to wait.

"We'll get our hook in that fellow yet," Xavier

promised Benito. "I'm going to get me some new kind of bait."

Meanwhile, urged on by the resident Portuguese adventurers, Benito took to sight-seeing, to admire for himself Kashmir's celebrated beauties. He first visited the capital, which, enthusiastic townsfolk assured him, had been founded by no less a personage than Solomon himself. The ruins of his palace, if proof were needed, still languished like bones on top of Tukt-i-Suliman, "Throne of Solomon." The legend was a foolish one and the "throne" an abrupt, ugly hill in Srinagar's environs. Each year crowds flocked to its summit to commemorate Solomon's wisdom and Kashmir's good fortune.

Benito saw the ruins for himself. He raised his foot and placed it against a rain-beaten square of granite and surveyed below him the scene Solomon never saw, the Kashmir Valley.

Tukt-i-Suliman rose in the Valley's center and Benito could see clearly in all directions, fifty miles to east and west and half as far in other directions, where snow-cropped mountains glistened like phantom back-drops. Climactic peaks towered above the fringe nine thousands of feet above the Valley floor and fifteen thousands above the sea. They were spectacular mountains. It was a spectacular Valley.

At Tukt-i-Suliman's base, Benito could examine the city bisected by its tree-banked river and surrounded with villas and lakes, on which fleets of sail-boats skimmed the waters, lightly, like flocks of giddy birds running in the wind. Broad avenues crossed town-squares at regular intervals, and parks and little bridges and monuments of many kinds marked the level of gentility at which the people had arrived.

Lovely Kashmir. Wherever one looked lay the stamp of shapeliness and beauty. It was a feast for one's eyes and Benito devoured it voraciously.

"Bihisht, bihisht," his guide hissed at his elbow. Indeed, thought Benito, it was "Bihisht," which meant to him and his companion, "Terrestrial Paradise." No where in India, surely, was there a panorama comparable to it.

In Srinagar's suburbs, Benito found a popular Hindu shrine. It consisted mostly of an elaborate series of pools for "sacred fish" which Akbar had built in his more orthodox days. A large spring flowed through birch trees and hazel brush into canals and finally into pools where the "Sacred" but canny trout loitered for choice bits tossed to them by pilgrims. Close by, a summer house nestled beneath chunar trees, monsters introduced from Persia by Akbar's ancestors. They were well-rounded, graceful trees with habits much like a chestnut, though far superior in trunk, bark, and foliage. The leaf looked like a maple and it turned brilliant red in autumn. Benito took a fancy to them and investigated possibilities of getting seeds to send his confreres in Goa.

"The Moguls will be remembered much longer for their chunar trees than their conquests," he said to the gardener who promised him a packet. The little old man bobbed his head and wondered what else to say to this serious stranger draped in somber black and topped with a hat like a mosque dome.

While the gardener fumbled, Benito tore a big leaf into bits without seeing its shape or color. His eyes held that dreamy, far-away look which accompanied his heavy moods and he spoke in a quiet monotone, "Boundaries shift like sands, but trees take root and flourish," he said.

"Yes, yes," said the old man eagerly. He knew what de Goes meant, for he could remember very well how the Great Mogul had captured the Valley many years before.

V

The summer, as it unfolded, proved to be an unusual one. Before June ended, farmers whom Benito met in the valley were complaining about drought.

"It looks bad," one said as his eyes swept the skies for rain clouds. "For two years now our rains have been stingy. We shall all starve." And he shrugged his shoulders indifferently, as if starving were not so bad as drought.

"Too long has Kashmir prospered," said another. "Famine is jealous and it will have our land too."

By late July the worst had to be admitted. Famine stalked the valley like an invisible assassin seaking vengeance for years of plenty. Crops withered and blew away. The land lay desolate, empty and scorched like a desert, and its people shriveled too. No help could come from the outside—mountain barriers might as well have been oceans without ships. What little there was the rich soon held, for the poor, being simple and generous, had not been able to make provision for the lean seasons.

Both Benito and Xavier did what they could to cheat the villain. With the king's favor and money they were able to provide where others could not, and all they managed to obtain was distributed to the poor. Every day they made the grim little journey across the lake to Srinagar, where they begged at the villas of the rich and wheedled a little from a little and managed somehow to prolong life in a few miserable bodies.

But it was pitifully inadequate. They saw hundreds die and hundreds dead, especially children, who feel first the weight of any affliction. They saw mothers cast their starving infants into road-side ditches and hastily retreat lest they be seen. They heard other mothers coaxing buyers right on the street.

"Do you want to buy a baby? Cheap, only a few rupees."

The Jesuits bought as many as they could, taking care to select those most in need, those beyond material help. For these they swung wide the pearly gates. "I baptize thee in the name of the Father, and of the Son, and of the Holy Ghost."

And after this there was always burial. Benito prepared tiny graves, and boxes that could serve as coffins. Xavier read prayers for Christian burial and blessed the fresh mounds of earth heaped up over the remains.

Fortunate little angels, they told one another, already flitting around heaven like butterflies. In the "Terrestrial Paradise," on the other hand, roads were piled high with corpses, people were famished and half-crazed, devouring human flesh like wolves, mourning and weeping at every hearth.

August and September passed in this way. Begging, baptizing, burying. They were dreadful months, but also consoling months, because priests take a certain consolation in their buryings. They are like doorkeepers who stand outside heaven's doors and give all who ask a gentle shove into that better world.

When early October came, the nights were bitter cold and the mornings too chilly for Akbar to stick his nose out of doors. All of the ducks had migrated. Instead, snow flurries flew about the up-lands and all the earth was barren and frosty.

From home Akbar had received news that his palace was partially rebuilt. "Enough room for the king, if not the court," the messenger had reported. Akbar was needed in Lahore, indeed urgently demanded by certain of the citizens who had much to lose in his absence.

And besides he was hungry. Even his normally frugal meals had been conditioned by the famine. It was surely time for him to give the orders for the return home, and he came up with them at last.

He wanted the Jesuits to be in his immediate attendance on the voyage, but they begged off. The hustle and bustle of court travel was too much for their devotions, they explained. Could they journey separately, then present themselves at the king's new residence in the capital?

By all means.

They piled an elephant high with movables, mounted their horses, and began their own descent down mountains like a colossal stair-case, through ice-bound valleys and the lion-skulking jungles. They arrived in Lahore on the thirteenth of November.

Father Emmanuel was on hand to greet them. Welcome, welcome! Had the trip been difficult?

Very. Road so rough their elephant had to use five legs.

Five legs? Oh, come now. . . .

No, honestly, the beast had put his trunk to the ground and steadied himself as with a staff.

The king? Oh, he'd be along shortly. In good spirits but more devoted to this sun-nonsense than ever before.

VI

In the summer of 1598, a wealthy Persian merchant appeared in Lahore and was directed to the court of the Grand Mogul. "I have come from Cathay," he announced.

Just by chance, Father Jerome Xavier was at court with Prince Salim when the Persian was introduced and questioned. Ah, here was sublime music for Jesuit ears!

"Yes," repeated the bagman of three-score years, "I have been to Cathay. Just now I'm returning from Mecca where I've been on pilgrimage. Before Mecca I was in Cathay."

"How long were you in Cathay?" the Prince inquired.

"Thirteen years, Your Majesty."

"And where did you live?"

"In the capital city, which is called Cambaluc. The king, whom I have seen many times, usually resides in that capital."

"This country, is it large?"

"Immense, Your Majesty." The Persian nodded gravely to add dimension to vast borders. "This kingdom has as many as fifteen hundred cities, all of them very populous."

"Is the king powerful?"

"He is a very mighty monarch. No one is ever allowed to address him except in writing. The king responds to these requests by means of couriers who deliver writings."

"How were you able to enter the country? Is this allowed to all?" Prince Salim coldly measured the adventurer, who was evidently enjoying every moment of his triumph.

"No, Your Majesty. I had gone there as Ambassador of the King of Kashgar. Notwithstanding my papers from this king, I was detained by the governor of the first frontier town till the king of Cathay had been informed of my arrival. A letter was brought to me from Cambaluc and I was allowed to continue my journey."

"Is the distance great?"

"Very great, but the journey was easily accomplished. We changed horses at each post and were thus able to travel from twenty-five to thirty leagues each day."

"Were you molested along the route by robbers?"

"No, Your Majesty. No, justice is very strictly applied in these regions and robbers are never pardoned. Hence we were free to travel without harm."

"What appearance and manners do the people of Cathay present?"

"Oh, I have never seen more handsome people. I prefer their appearance to either the Greeks or the Turks. The men wear long beards, and both men and women are light-complexioned."

"What of their religion?"

Father Jerome bent more closely. The conversation was in Persian; and though the Father easily spoke this tongue, he had to listen carefully.

"For the most part they are followers of Isauitae, that is to say, of Jesus."

"Are all these people, then, Christians?" Prince Salim asked.

"By no means. Many are Mussauites, that is followers of Moses, and others are Mohammedans."

"And their king, is he a Mohammedan?"

69

"Not yet," answered the Persian, drawing himself up stiffly, "but it is hoped that he will become one soon."

At this point Prince Salim was interrupted by other business. "The Father," he jerked his head toward Xavier, "is very interested in these matters. Can you return in a few days to tell us more about Cathay?"

A day was fixed and the merchant bowed his way out.

That night, sleep didn't come to Father Jerome. Nor prayer. Only visions of Cathay and fifteen-hundred populous cities. Schemes, schemes. Pious plots to land himself in Cambaluc.

His Jesuit community was in uproar. Here was the opportunity of centuries. Whose would it be?

Mine, thought Father Emmanuel, if I can get away from this parish.

Mine, Xavier reasoned, if I can get away from court.

And Benito? Benito scarcely hoped.

Too excited to await the appointed day, Father Jerome sought out the Persian in his lodgings. He was sorry, he told the merchant, to anticipate their conversation. Unhappily he knew no peace till he heard more of Cathay. Was it true that in Cathay there were many followers of Jesus?

"Yes," old long-whiskers replied, "I was intimately acquainted with many of them."

"What of their churches?"

"They have many churches, some very large. On the walls are pictures, some painted, some prints on paper. Most are in colors. In one church I saw a painting of your crucified Jesus. It was much reverenced by the people."

"Are there priests in these churches?"

"Yes, there is a priest at each church. The people pay great respect to them and bring them presents."

70

"Do they have bishops in Cathay?"

The merchant didn't know what a bishop was. "Oh yes," he said after Xaxier explained, "certainly some of the priests are superior to others."

"How do the priests dress?"

"They wear black robes like yours, and bonnets on their heads very like yours, but a little larger."

Yes, the king was a Christian. He supported student priests and often went to church. There were many amongst the Christians, both men and women, who lived secluded lives and never married.

With hopes star-high, Father Jerome reported every detail to superiors in Goa. He was careful to add that, though the merchant could be mistaken (merchants were born liars), the matter should at least be investigated. Perhaps, he suggested, someone should make a journey from Lahore, since the route to Cathay was but a short one.

For Benito de Goes a mighty destiny was about to be born. As yet it lay lightly, as in the darkness of the womb. No one knew of it save God, who had given it life.

VII

Before the spring of 1601 Akbar subjugated the land of the Deccans, but he wasn't satisfied. More lands, more kingdoms, more tribute were the tunes constantly dinning in his ears. He began now to speak openly of war with the Portuguese. He would have all their possessions, he bragged. It was a simple matter. Let others but wait— they would see for themselves.

It so happened that a former Portuguese soldier, outlawed from his barracks for mischief, happened to be present when Akbar was raving in this fashion. He begged the Mogul's permission to say what was in his mind.

"By all means," said Akbar.

"Your Majesty appears to be very confident," the Portuguese said, "but as we say in my country, there is such a thing as reckoning without one's host. If the Portuguese are as brave as you've often said they are, do you think you can get the better of them so easily? Why even if they were only chickens, they would surely peck before being caught!"

"I have no intention of fighting hand to hand," retorted the king. "I'll overcome them by hunger."

"Excellent!" snapped the soldier. "You've got the same idea they have. They intend to conquer you by thirst!"

"Bravo!" cried Akbar. He thought the fellow very witty and made much of him before the others. But he changed his crafty plans not a bit.

On occasion he sent his ambassadors to Goa. These "good-will" tours were carefully timed with Portuguese fleet arrivals, and Akbar's ambassador-agents had strict orders to spy out imported goods, ship and man-power, fortifications, and other related data.

For espionage, then, Akbar planned an embassy in 1601. The alleged object of this mission was two-fold: a peace alliance with the Portuguese, and information regarding a Mogor deputation to Portugal. Akbar glibly talked of sending presents to the Pope and King of Portugal and he wanted Goa's official opinion on protocol.

Surely, he confided to his secretary, this would put him in good standing.

He fished around for a suitable Portuguese to accompany his expedition.

"Brother de Goes!" he cried. The inspiration was divine. He sent for the Jesuit.

Benito came, climbed up to the royal cushions, and scolded Akbar for hours. "You are foxing no one," he told the disconcerted Mogul. "This war is all foolishness and God will punish you for it."

At length Akbar was convinced. The proposed war was all foolishness and he solemnly promised Benito that he would drop it like a scorpion. But, he declared, the embassy to Goa must in any case be completed and Benito must accompany it. As a token of his regard for Benito, he presented him a host of half-caste slaves, descendants of Portuguese ne'er-do-wells. One happened to be a Jew more than ninety years old. "These," Akbar said to Benito, "you can take with you to Goa. They are yours."

May days were dawning when the legation reached Goa. It was met at the city walls by an imposing array of European nobility decked out in all its medals and ribbons and velvets. There were soldiers, sporty horses, camels, and richly caparisoned elephants, carts and plenty of dogs. Through the city streets it paraded to the booming of artillery and hurrahs of townspeople. Gun salutes on Goa Island and in the city continued throughout the day—the Portuguese had a message to convey and they were assuring its reception. Akbar's ambassador, Benito soon discovered, fully appreciated the significance of this music.

When the parading was concluded, an audience was granted by the viceroy. An official, puffing importantly, preceded the legation into the vice-regal reception hall, and after all had taken the places assigned them, someone

73

began to read in a ringing, almost unintelligible voice. He was done up in striped red and gold and for all the world looked like a tulip.

"The message of the great lord of the law of Mohammed, high and mighty king, slayer of hostile kings, to whom the great pay homage, whose dignity is unsurpassed, who is exalted above other kings and whose government is renowned throughout the world, to Ayres de Saldagna Viceroy."

The "tulip" gasped for breath and started with new vigor.

"Meeting with favor and grace at the hands of the king of kings, honored and privileged by him, know that, by the grace of God, all the ports of Hindustan, from Cinde to Chatigan and Pegu, are under our high prosperity; and it is always in our royal heart and before our eyes, that the rich merchants and those who traffic may be able to go and come with all assurance and safety, so that they may continually pray to God for the increase of our prosperity, and especially the inhabitants of the kingdoms of the Portuguese, who, outside this kingdom, cannot go and come freely, and who are accustomed to navigate the sea of Hindustan.

"For this reason our royal honor has willed and arranged that one of our servants and courtiers has been sent as an ambassador to confirm once again the basis of the alliance, so that there may henceforth be no occasion to doubt it. On this occasion the Brother Benito de Goes has been sent together with our trusted servant Cogetqui Soldan Hama to your parts. . . .

"And if there are any skilled craftsmen who desire to visit our royal court, which is like the mansions of the blest, he shall give them all that they need in food and apparel, and bring them with him to this, our court, the

74

fulcrum of the world, on the understanding that, having been in our service, they shall have leave to return to their country whenever it shall be their will to do so. . . .

"As to other matters, our ambassador will make them known to you by word of mouth.

"The ninth day of Fauardi of God, of the forty-sixth year of the era."

After Akbar's modest claims had been heard, if not listened to, Soldan Hama stepped forth, and bowing absurdly low, begged for the privilege of making gifts to his excellency the Viceroy. Then he bowed again in that extreme fashion and his servants lugged in several thick Kashmir carpets. The vice-regal eyes sparkled with the richness of them, though he tried to act indifferent, as if he had Kashmir rugs by the hundreds in his bedroom and parlor.

A panther on a gold leash was introduced. "For the chase," Soldan Hama commented, then a smaller panther, which was really a cheetah. Finally (the Viceroy had to take the legate's word for it), there was a horse, "celestial and fearless charger, direct lineal descendant of Bucephalus, noble mount of Alexander, once ruler of Macedonia and Emperor of the East." Of course the "celestial" horse didn't appear: it was too busy at that moment eating just ordinary hay, along with Portuguese horses of humbler origin.

More valuable in Benito's eyes were the gifts he himself ushered in, his small army of half-castes. With the dignity of a mitred abbot and a grave little speech he presented them, and the viceroy was visibly touched.

"When you convert them, Brother," he said, "I shall stand as godfather to them."

And he did.

75

VIII

When Benito returned as imperial legate, Goa was about the same. "New Lisbon" the Portuguese East called its port and the saying was current that, seeing Goa, one saw Lisbon. From quays along the river-waterfront sailors could observe a sea of red tiled roofs glowing in the sun. Here and there tufts of palm trees cropped up and church belfries marked the limits of God's domain in the settlement.

Goa was cosmopolitan. The whole East dumped its restless there and Goa contained them. From Tartary and Brao came impassive midgets with mere slits for eyes and long pigtails braided to serpents' thinness and dangling down backs or coiled conspicuously in side pockets. Tall Arabs were there, in turbans and cabaia. Doctors from Venice. Jews in gabardine, ebony-black Kaffirs and Malays, fat, complacent Guzaratis. White men, black men, brown men. Up and down the Rua Direita they surged, all intent on one thing, a more-than-equal share in the fruits of the Orient. For at Goa, East met East and East met West in a ceaseless barter for advantage. Profit. What else mattered?

The hot streets were one incessant carnival. Umbrellas like beds of mushrooms covered crawling things and dark business and struggle for survival. Cheating, quarreling, killing, only occasionally some honesty.

In more respectable and permanent chambers Lombardian bankers counted their moneys and exchanged coins from every country of the world. Goldsmiths exhibited their skill. Flemish merchants traded fine fabrics and tapestries. Bengalese muslins, thin as gauze, lay on shop counters. Corals brought down by Arabs, pearls from Pescaria and gold dust from Sofala; rubies, diamonds gathered in dreamy, mystic lands on the fringe of the unknown; fine Chinese silks and porcelain like eggshell: all these and more were displayed in bazaars to coax profit from buyers.

And buyers flocked to the coaxing. Like patrons of public swindlers they struggled to perpetuate that miserable profit. "Oh, son of a pig!" they hissed at one another, "let me pass." And they pushed and elbowed and shouted their entrance into Mammon's temples to seek rest for their souls in baubles. Without knowing it, they were looking for God. They were shouting for God, sinning perhaps, to find the happiness only God could give. Such are humans everywhere and such was Goa.

To de Goes, Goa had a deeper significance. It was the Rome of Eastern Christianity. Church officials ruled from its church thrones, and their edicts or fulminations penetrated the continent, the sub-continent, and a thousand islands. The headquarters of the Jesuits, too, were here. Here Father Francis Xavier was entombed, and here Benito had made his novitiate as a Jesuit. Goa was a heart pumping energy into the body. But it was also a hearth where the body retrieved its strength and warmed at the fires of comradeship.

Though a man of some pretensions as legate of the Slayer of Hostile Kings, Benito slipped easily into his place in the Goa Jesuit community. In short order he was assigned to help serve community needs, tasks like putting plates on the table and taking them off again. Among those benefited by this lordly service of the legate was Father Nicolas Pimenta, official Visitor of the Jesuit General in Rome. Father Nicolas had come

77

to make observations for another, but he had ended up by staying as superior.

He was a man of vision. Though conservatively middle-aged, he was fired with the imagination of an explorer, or youthful conqueror like Alexander of Macedonia. Like all mortals, he suffered somewhat from the prejudices of his times. He placed his confidence in a book called the *Theatrum Orbis Terrarum*, which was a highly respectable, though not very reliable, atlas of Orselius, published in Antwerp in 1570 when Father Nicolas was just twenty-four in years. It epitomized the geographical knowledge and errors of the era. Among other wonders, it put that great land of fable, Cathay, to the northwest of China. There it was for all to see, "Cathay."

Cathay, just a few leagues away! Could this be true? He, Father Nicolas, was in a position to command. If Cathay were there, as Orselius said it was, then the Jesuit superior would know of it before he laid his bones down for the last time.

Let it not be said that Father Nicolas allowed himself to be carried away by hopes. Far from it. He was conscious of his responsibility both to his Order and to his Church. He knew he was an instrument of Providence in the administration of a portion of that Church. He would have to answer for it. At his elbow he had such and such evidence. Not far distant was the lost Atlantis of Marco Polo with its vast number of Christians waiting for a Papal legate to reunite them to the one fold. Could Father Nicolas ignore that?

What was the evidence? First there was the *Theatrum Orbis*. The superior considered it more closely. Now, a map was a map. Its significance lay in its power to expose, to direct. One need not have verified it by

78

personal observation, for this would be a denial of the nature of a map. One didn't accept every map as a dogma of the holy faith, but still, maps were maps produced with much labor and erudition by experts in the field. Irrefutable logic.

"Cathay" to the northwest of China, north and west of Peking where Father Ricci lived. How long the route from Mogul India? Six months, someone had said. "Three months' journey," said the *Theatrum*, "lies between the borders of Cathay and its capital, Cambaluc." Six months to the Cathayan borders, three months to the capital. Why, the journey was but a brief one!

To contradict all this, Father Nicolas had the testimony of Ricci himself. In 1596, the latter had written to the General in Rome that he was absolutely certain China was identical with Cathay. His letter and theory were well known among the brethren in India. It was the one piece of evidence that didn't fit in. Now Father Nicolas wanted all to know that he respected Ricci. He didn't say Ricci was wrong. His theory was simply a part of the puzzle that had no place. Especially this in view of Father Jerome Xavier's opinions.

Father Jerome had much to say in the matter. Too much. For him facts were lacking, but nothing could be surer than the existence of Cathay six months' journey from Mogor India, as certain as the tides, and the full moon when it was due. Had he not talked with certain persons who but lately had themselves been in Cathay? Let Ricci stick to numbers, and Father Jerome would produce Cathay right out of the enveloping mists.

In a letter hastily scribbled July 26, 1598, Xavier reported to his superior in great detail. In August, 1599, he undertook another thundering account to jar the superior into action. He had questioned traders about routes. Through Tibet, that was the shortest. Through Tibet to Kashgar, whence it was but a short distance to the first town of Cathay, which, the merchants avowed, was Christian.

Just how was one to achieve Tibet from Lahore, center of Mogor India? Xavier didn't explain. Since no European had yet scaled its mountain passes on trails not much wider than a man's two fists, Xavier was in no position to explain.

Nor could he say how foreigners were to coax passports from isolationist Tibet. But the merchants—they reported this and that! They swore it by the Prophet's beard. Surely here was evidence, if honest evidence was wanted.

That the merchants were wholly deceived, neither Xavier nor Father Nicolas could know. Though Eastern merchants have established for themselves reputations as professional liars, Xavier's friends undoubtedly meant well and thought themselves truthful in all they related. They had confused Buddhists with Christians, not a shameful mistake withal, for Vasco da Gama and all his men had actually prayed before a Buddhist idol at Calicut thinking it to be a Madonna with Christ-child. The merchant's armies of Christians were really Chinese Buddhists; their Christian seminaries, prosperous and populous, were Buddhist monasteries. As for the hats, like Xavier's only a little larger, they may have been Christian head-gear, but they certainly rested on Buddhist heads.

Father Nicolas believed the merchants. He himself spoke Persian fluently, and perhaps this gave him kinship and sympathy for the Persian merchants. Xavier, who vouched for their veracity, had a fine reputation in his Order. Surely there was no obvious reason why his opinions should be disregarded. So, cautiously, Father Nicolas believed him too.

As a final and nifty piece of evidence, there was de Goes. The superior had become well acquainted with him these several months. His reserve, his good judgment, his unfailing response in all that was easy or difficult, his facility in languages stamped him as reliable.

Had Providence placed this Jesuit Marco Polo right under the superior's nose as an indication of its decision? Were the Jesuits just slow or over-cautious instruments in the hands of Providence? The superior wished he knew.

Send a mission, cried Xavier. There was no Cathay, said Ricci. Cathay northwest of China, explained the *Theatrum Orbis*. What did the Brother say? He declined to comment. But he was prepared to do what he was told, he said, and nothing would give him greater satisfaction.

After these preliminaries, Father Nicolas wrote to Spain's Philip III, who was also King of Portugal at this time. He wrote to the Jesuit General in Rome that he had written to Philip III. "His Majesty wants us to go," he told the General, "and he has ordered his viceroy to help defray expenses." Then he added that Father Xavier had approached the Great Akbar for approval and letters of credit. Akbar had cried out, "Rahmat-i-Khuda" which meant: "God's blessing be upon you!" and had given voice to other words of praise. He insisted on presenting Brother de Goes with four hundred gold pieces, which four hundred gold pieces would come in mighty handy.

The plan, Father Nicolas continued, was this: Brother de Goes and Father Machado were to leave for Agra where Akbar now held court and where Father Xavier awaited his pleasure. At Agra passports would be provided, a retinue gathered, and the final touches made. Thence the party would proceed to Lahore, to Kabul, Badakshan, and Tartary. The Tibet route had been abandoned because it was found to be "difficult." The roads through Kabul, Badakshan, and central Asia, though longer, were assuredly easier and better known. Father Xavier, after much diligence, had uncovered these details. Would His Reverence, the General, have prayers said for the success of this journey?

When the weary business was done for, Father Nicolas prepared another dispatch for Ricci. It was brief, to the point, and would go via Macao the following spring. Two Jesuits were on their way. Ricci could expect them after they had contacted the Cathayans. Probably within two years they would arrive at Peking.

Father Nicolas sent for Brother de Goes a last time. The latter answered the summons with an aching heart. Would he see this man again, this Father of his soul?

"Brother," the superior began, "I have sent for you to give you my blessing." He was a Latin; he wanted to weep like a Latin. It was a hard thing to send a son to probable death. How much easier to go oneself!

But one must do hard things for Christ's cause, and one must not be melodramatic about it. There was no place for sentiment between two men who had long since offered their lives.

"Brother, you are prepared to go?" the superior's voice was matter-of-fact now, kind but businesslike.

"Yes, Your Reverence."

"You realize, of course, what it means?"

"Yes, Your Reverence."

"We must not maximize the dangers," the priest said hopefully, "nor must we minimize them. Your greatest cross will be the absence of Mass and Holy Communion. But we must not be spiritual gluttons, eager for more than God wants us to have. I will keep you in my prayers till we hear that you have returned safely."

Benito knelt at his superior's feet.

"May the blessing of God, of the Father, the Son, and the Holy Ghost descend upon you and remain forever." And the priest tenderly pressed his hands down on the bowed head. "God speed," he whispered when he bent over. "Make haste to Peking."

I X

In lovely old Peking, Father Mathew Ricci went about his business of numbers and clocks (and as time allowed, geography) wholly undisturbed by the Jesuit storms on India's sub-continent. His apartments, located "in the gardens," were adjacent to quarters made available for visitors of renown and foreign embassies. It was a fortunate arrangement, for it allowed him intimate contact with these "ambassadors" of the lands to the west.

Father Mathew was not taken in by their ambassadorial rank. For that matter, neither was the Emperor, nor any one at the court. These latter worthies were much too proud to admit what was true and what everyone in Asia knew. The Emperor of China liked to consider himself the sun of a system, that principle of light and heat which made possible all advantage of lesser bodies. Foreign merchants took profit from this colossal vanity, and after faking credentials as ambassadors from this or that kingdom, they flocked to the imperial court to render homage. Of course, they fetched gifts, gifts as extravagant as their purses afforded, for the Emperor considered it beneath his dignity to accept without a sevenfold return. And thus merchants everywhere looked on Peking as the El Dorado, and the Emperor a gold mint where one could clear enough profit to retire from bales and barter.

Father Mathew knew all this well, but he tactfully kept it to himself. Instead of despising them as impostors, he passed among these illustrious legates and interested himself in the lands of their beginnings. In this fashion he had long since concluded that the *Theatrum Orbis* was a fake, too, at least insofar as Cathay was concerned.

During the portentous year of 1601, indeed while Goa's Father Superior bustled with energy to set the Cathay-mission into motion, Father Mathew became acquainted with certain of these ambassadors from India. Their leader was a vigorous, hearty Armenian whose most conspicuous feature was his beard. Such a beard! Prolific, well groomed, perfumed with just the right shade of manliness. "Si-Ma-Teou," as everyone in the capital called Ricci, came to know the beard's strokings, tender, loving touches when its master was in an expansive mood.

Yes, the merchants had passed through the realms of Grand Mogul. When was that? The "beard" swished toward a subordinate whose eyes peered suspiciously across a huge parrot-beak of a nose. Two, three years, maybe four. What difference did it make? Yes, they had heard there were "Black Devils," foreign monks who went by the names of Padres, somewhere in Akbar's service. Not very popular with the people; in fact they'd long since have been dispatched if Akbar hadn't protected them.

Akbar? Oh, he'd been conducting a campaign against

84

the Deccan. His son, the drinking son, had fallen from his horse and died in that war. Some kind of fit, perhaps drunk. Yes, there were reports of Akbar's success. "Fortunate as Akbar" was a popular saying. Yes, the honorable ambassadors planned a return to India as soon as current business was brought to issue. Tedious business, this diplomacy. The trail was long. So long a voyage into the rising sun was scarcely worth while. Now, wasn't that the truth?

The merchants were not slow in discovering that Si-Ma-Teou was a personage of considerable repute. They heard on all sides about his singular gifts to the Emperor: clocks, clavichords, and paintings of other lands. Lords and princes spoke in the highest terms of his number-words and learned men from all parts of the kingdom listened while he explained the Christian law.

There came a time when the merchants were scheduled to leave Peking. They visited Si-Ma-Teou a last time with expressions of regret and respect. Then, as they proceeded along his garden walk, one noticed several pieces of writing paper, evidently cast aside by the learned teacher or one of his servants.

"Ah, just the thing," the bearded Armenian said to himself, and he stooped to gather the papers in. "I shall take these to my friends in India to show them what kind of writing is in use among strangers."

He tucked his souvenirs carefully in a packet of credentials and turned his beard to the west.

85

PART 3. THE CABAIA

I

$\mathcal{A}$ T THE age of forty, in his twelfth year of Jesuit life, Brother Benito de Goes put on a disguise. It was like dying without being buried. His Jesuit cassock was tucked away, his shirts and trousers were boxed with other valueless remnants, until, perchance, he might return again to the old life, to live again with his confreres.

Before the break with the past came, Benito made his preparations to "die" well and to stay "dead" long. He darkened his hair and skin. He grew a bushy beard. He gathered garments and accessories to the new life, not harps nor halos, but things like swords and rings and a turban.

This strange metamorphosis, in which one personality was to perish and another emerge, took place in the Mogul city of Agra. Akbar had returned there after the Deccan campaign, and with him, Father Jerome Xavier, the chief designer of Benito's new life.

If de Goes lacked enthusiasm for the project, Xavier did not, and at the moment that's all that mattered. For Xavier carried others with him, particularly when his was the responsibility for steering the course. De Goes had been ordered to report to him for briefing.

Benito had arrived at Agra in the company of Father

Anthony Machado, and Xavier, brisk as a baker, began the instructions. Machado, he decided, was to remain in Agra to study the Persian and Turkish tongues. Benito was to go ahead to reconnoitre. When the ground had been carefully laid and Cathay was at least within range, he was to come back for the Father and they would return to the Cathayans together. In the event that Cathay was closer to China than India, he was to present his credentials to the Christian authorities in Cambaluc, then proceed to Peking and report to Father Ricci.

The route planned by Xavier was the most formidable imaginable, although, it must be admitted, Xavier knew too little about it to realize that. No European had successfully negotiated it for over three hundred years, not since Marco Polo. None, except Brother Benito, would succeed in traversing it for another three hundred years, not till Victorian England. The road lay through strongholds of fanatic Mohammedans, through the dizzy passes and plateaus of the Himalayas, through the Takla Makan and Gobi deserts, into the Great Wall of China, and so to Peking.

Cathay, according to Xavier's optimistic calculations, would be somewhere in the unknown void between the Himalayas and the Great Wall. The rest was for Brother Benito to discover. He should proceed north to Lahore, in the guise of a Persian merchant, taking care to avoid Jesuits lest his identity be revealed. At Lahore he should join a caravan to Yarkand. After Yarkand, the route was anybody's guess; not even Xavier's fertile imagination could produce the road beyond.

There was the plan. Finding Cathay would be as simple as finding Father Jerome's biretta. And Benito was satisfied to let the plan go at that.

He began its execution with the disguise, a trying

90

operation, for the Jesuit in him died slowly—as slowly as his beard grew—and the Persian merchant who replaced him emerged just as reluctantly. But he did finally come forth, a stocky figure in the cabaia and turban of the Moor, with a great red sash at his middle. To support the role, he collected an assortment of pack camels complete with burdens of convincing bulk and, finally, a merchant's retinue. Father Jerome provided six trusty travelling companions: Leon Grimon, a sub-deacon who spoke Turkish and Persian, a merchant called Demetrius, and four servants.

Grimon the sub-deacon was an old friend of the Jesuits as well as Akbar's. He was a man of great intelligence and had seen many things, and Akbar was so pleased with his conversation that he employed him as ambassador. On one occasion he had sent him with letters and gifts to the Jesuits in Goa to coax them back to his court. This was in 1590, shortly after Father Rudolph had left Akbar high and dry in his religious scruples.

It was solely on account of his affection for the Jesuits that Grimon consented to accompany de Goes. To do so, he had to sacrifice his handsome salary (one crusado a day) which he received from Akbar, and what was much more, his wife, to whom he had been recently married.

Benito concluded his preparations by paying Akbar a visit. The Great Mogul roared his pleasure on seeing him in the guise of a shrewd money-maker.

"That turban," he said playfully, "needs more jewels. Now you leave it to me. I'll have you done up like the Great Shah of Persia."

Akbar insisted that Benito take his old place on the royal dais and there he plied him with questions and attentions. Something to drink? Some tobacco to smoke?

91

In the Deccan, Akbar had been introduced to smoking and didn't quite know what to make of it. "Is it against the Christian law to smoke?" he asked.

Benito laughed.

"Why do you laugh?"

"Some one else just asked me the same thing." Benito screwed up his face, like a judge about to give a difficult decision. "What is all this fuss about smoking?"

"No fuss," said Akbar, "but I've a mind to forbid its use. It's degrading—and extravagant besides. I don't want my people to import it."

Benito laughed again. Smoking tobacco was degrading —coming from Akbar that was a good one! "Oh no," he said, "the Christian law doesn't forbid tobacco. Smoke all you want."

Akbar pretended to be angry. "Be serious," he said gruffly.

True to his word, Akbar provided de Goes with gold pieces and passports, grandiloquent passports, that for elegance and bravado should have turned back all the foes of Asia. He, the Slayer of Hostile Kings, would have everyone know that the bearer was an intimate friend of his, that he was to be treated with great respect and generosity, that he was to be exempt from all taxes including local tolls, and finally that any harm done to him would be followed by certain and speedy vengeance. So speaketh the Slayer of Hostile Kings.

Moreover, to back up this eloquence, he insisted that de Goes be accompanied by two hundred imperial troops. The latter were to become attached to the expedition when it left Lahore.

"Rahmat-i-Khuda!" cried Akbar when Benito bade farewell. "God's blessing be upon you!"

By October twenty-eighth all was in readiness. Benito

92

spent that entire night discussing the journey with Fathers Xavier and Machado, and the next morning, after an early Mass, without ceremony, speeches, or breakfast even, he mounted his horse, waved goodbye, and turned north to Lahore.

"God be with you," were Xavier's last words. "We'll be waiting for you though it be twenty years!"

It was dark yet and the horses's hoofs echoed solemnly in Agra's empty streets. Like Xavier's words echoing in Benito's heart.

". . . though it be twenty years."

I I

John Galiseo was a Venetian, like Marco Polo, and a busier one nobody could imagine. He conducted a going business in imports, mostly foodstuffs like dried fruits from the Gulf area; and his caravans, like so many fleets, sailed into vast seas of sand throughout southeastern Asia and returned with cargoes that brought princes to his door.

They also brought Jesuits to his door. Especially one, Father Emmanuel Pinheiro, who came nearly every day to beg for his poor-box. Galiseo would tell you (as he often told others) that Father Emmanuel was a "saint," meaning by this that Father Emmanuel's gaiety filled Lahore's dark slums like a purifying sunshine. For the Venetian that was sanctity—laughter in the slums to dispel the vapors of misery, even the misery "of those pig-headed infidels."

Just this morning Galiseo had dispatched a donkey to the priest's house, a donkey loaded down with two bulging bags, rice and barley, one hanging over each side. He knew that the beast would soon return with a note tied to its bridle, because that was Father Emmanuel's way of saying "Thank You."

"I send the ass back to you, laden with God's blessings. Pinheiro, S.J."

Galiseo treasured those notes. He kept them like banknotes, all counted out and tied in little bundles. Some day, he often told himself, he would use them to pay his way into heaven, to save time and red-tape getting into that paradise after the present one had to be abandoned. "Money gets anything," he would say; "my money is immortal."

At the moment the Venetian had a task to perform for his "saint." He lighted a candle from the hearth and poked about his desk for a quill. It was like digging up some ancient artifact in a mound of clutterings. He found one, dipped it into ink, and patiently scratched Emmanuel's name across the top of the page. Then he cocked his head lightly, to examine what he had written. Apparently satisfied, he turned over the page and scratched again.

"He is here," he wrote; "come tonight at eleven-thirty."

Just that, then his name, "John Galiseo."

He cupped his hands and clapped a couple of times. The door swung wide and a black little fellow stood there, grinning and eager. The master tipped handsomely; tonight, perhaps, there would be a great tip.

"Take this to the Padri's." Galiseo folded it and held the candle under the ruddy red sealing wax till a glob dropped where he wanted it. He blew out the candle with a hurricane puff and papers on his desk fluttered, helpless against the wind. "The Padri's. You know?"

The boy nodded and disappeared.

Galiseo left, too, to ask his guest if anything was needed before the morrow.

At precisely eleven-thirty on that night of December eighth, an excited Father Emmanuel Pinheiro and a calm Father Francis Corsi were introduced to a mysterious Persian, whose turban glistened conspicuously, like Akbar's crown.

"Brother Benito!" Emmanuel cried. "Why this is like a novel—a Jesuit in disguise and all that!"

"Sh-h-h-h!" said Benito, putting his finger to his lips. His ring sparkled like the turban. "You know—I'm the Abdullah now." In jest he assumed his role, an obsequious pose and the expressionless Oriental face. "Your *most* humble servant, Abdullah Isai," and he bowed absurdly low.

"My eyes gleam with joy at your arrival," said Emmanuel with another sweep to the floor. "I hope you are not tired."

"My foot on your eye!" answered Benito. It was a climax to the politeness.

Everybody laughed at this buffoonery; then Emmanuel was busy admiring Benito's costume.

"It's beautiful," he said enviously. "You've shed the old like a—a butterfly winging its way across the world!"

"Yes, yes," said Benito, not impressed by this flight of fancy. "Let's get down to business . . . we haven't much time." He tossed his turban into the corner. "I must get rid of the four servants. They talk too much—do nothing."

"Very well." Emmanuel tried his best to appear grave and efficient. "Shall I get you others?"

"Only one, a good one," said Benito, accenting the "good" like a canonization. "And a Christian, if you please!"

95

Galiseo, who had just returned, offered to produce one. "I have an Armenian called Isaac."

"That friendly little midget who just got married?" asked Father Corsi.

"The very one. He is loyal and generous. We can depend on him."

"I've known him for years," Emmanuel said. "We are good friends. Just the man."

No one thought of asking Isaac's wife what *she* thought. After all, caravaneers were like sea captains or sailors; it was taken for granted that their marriages would be interrupted for interminable spells. A hard age for women.

"When will you leave for Kabul?" asked Emmanuel.

"No caravan till after the New Year. February, maybe." He shrugged. "I suppose I'm stuck here till then . . . if only I could go to Mass. . . ."

They were all saddened by Benito's loneliness for his God in the Eucharist.

"Sundays," said Emmanuel, pulling on his great black cape. "We needn't recognize one another—no one will know."

While Benito fetched his hat, Emmanuel lapsed into abstractions. He appeared to be sorting his ideas, folding them and packing them in a little bag. "Let's go," he said, when he had closed the receptacle, and he shoved out of the door with Father Corsi in tow.

Christmas came and passed and de Goes was still in residence at the Venetian's. Though he appreciated the room and roof offered him, he scarcely liked it as a lodging. Not that it was just noisy—he had once sought noise for its own sake. Noise is external to man and can be ignored like rain or snowfall. But one's own thoughts cannot. Benito discovered now as never before that he could not readily shed what passed through his mind during the day. His thinking was becoming of necessity increasingly mundane. His disguise demanded it, constant talk of buying and selling and news of the trail.

This was bad enough, but worse still was the barrage of profanity and vulgarity that he was daily subjected to. At first it was difficult to conceal his anger and to keep out of fights—the soldier in him had not yet been killed.

"I am Abdullah *Isai*," he would say, his temper rising with every inflection. "A Christian does not tolerate such talk."

Sometimes he received the obvious retort that Christians were often heard using such talk. But in general his views came to be respected. They came to accept him as "odd," one who refused to discuss sex or amorous conquests.

At the end of the year 1602, full of weariness and heartache, he undertook his first report to the superior at Goa. There he sat, a pathetic figure in silks and jewels, in the flickering open lamp-light, writing a letter he himself could not bear to read.

"Very Reverend and dear Father," he wrote, "it has pleased God to bring me to this city of Lahore, whence I am about to start for the country of Cathay. I should be neglecting my bounden duty if I departed without first writing to bid farewell to Your Reverence and my beloved Brothers in the lands of the South. I bade farewell to Father Jerome Xavier and Father Anthony Machado at Agra on the 29th of October. When I parted from them, I parted also from the dress I was wearing, exchanging it for the costume of the country in which I am now attired. I will not attempt to tell Your Reverence what my feelings were when I saw

97

myself in these strange garments. When they came to see me for the last time, Father Xavier and Father Anthony Machado remained with me the whole night giving me advice and instruction. It was with a sorrowful heart that I took leave of them and set out for Lahore. On the way some took me for a Saiyid, which means a descendant of Mohammed, and others for a grandee of the kingdom of Mecca; but they little knew the school in which I had been brought up. May God be praised for all his blessings.

"I arrived at Lahore on the 8th of December. I made my arrival known to Father Emmanuel Pinheiro and Father Corsi, but did not go to their house, as I had been instructed not to do so. Father Emmanuel Pinheiro came to see me, being much concerned that he could not entertain me, as is the custom of our Company. I am staying in the house of a Venetian named John Galiseo, where I am playing the part of a merchant. To make my disguise more complete, I am wearing a beard reaching to my breast, and long hair, as is the fashion amongst these people. All this, my Father, I am doing for the love of the Lord, who so greatly loveth us, and suffered for us. I beg Your Reverence after reading this to say a Mass for me to Our Lady of Victory, that she may enable me to triumph over all my enemies and difficulties; and I beg the same of all the Fathers and Brothers of these parts. They know well that those amongst whom I am going are wolves, the arch enemies of our Faith; but I go confident that I have their prayers.

"I am now known as Abdullah Isai, that is, 'Servant of Jesus,' a name which Father Jerome Xavier gave to me when we parted. The seal on this letter is made with the ring which, following the custom of the country, I now wear on my finger. The King has been very generous to me. He has furnished me with many of the necessities for my journey, and has also paid me for the whole time that I was in India. With this money, amounting to more than a thousand rupees, the Fathers have paid off some debts, and I have defrayed the cost of my journey from India to Agra. May God make his Majesty a Christian, which is the greatest good we can desire for him in this life. It remains only for me to send my greetings to Your Reverence and to the Fathers and Brothers in those parts. May the peace of Jesus Christ be with them and with you. Amen. From Lahore, the 30th December, 1602."

Benito's letter was read in many a pulpit before it was finally filed away in a dusty archive.

I I I

It is February 24, 1603. Abdullah Isai with his three companions and some two hundreds of soldiers stand on the banks of the river Ravi and peer into the shadows beyond. Across the sweeping waters a caravan awaits their arrival. It will leave soon for the fabulous regions of Badakshan and Turkestan and Tartary; Abdullah with escort is to companion it.

An expectant hush attends the vigil, for the tongues of men move reluctantly in the early morn, and before danger not at all. Harness-metal tinkles softly. Cocks crowing from distant roosts sound like bugles demanding instant service in battle. Even the stupid cart-oxen sense it and they chomp nervously on their cuds and turn heavy shoulders apprehensively.

Men have pulled their cloaks of silence about their

ears. They pace. They beat their arms like athletes during a warm-up. They brood. For here there are no dock crowds to cheer them off like sailors going to sea. Only chilly stillness and waiting. Waiting for fire-signals from the caravan, for the cold splashing waters of the riverford, waiting for battle. . . .

One, just one, stirs in business, and all watch him with affected indifference. It is the Abdullah, who gravely wags a big head and a black flowing beard that reaches down to his chest. One would never suspect his Portuguese beginnings, for to all who examine him, he is Persian. A swarthy Persian merchant decked out in acres of cabaia, a jewel-crusted turban and belt-sword, besides a bow with arrows. He makes a grand display of wealth and sagacity. Questionable virtues attributed to questionable Eastern merchants. He nods. He consults. He estimates his bags and pack camels. He is an actor. He carries off his part well and nobody suspects anything.

Abdullah's companions have taken less pains to disguise themselves. There is Grimon, whose silk garments drop in folds, almost like a bishop's, though not so full or resplendent. There is Demetrius, who is conspicuous for his height. But no one would deny that he was Greek, not even Demetrius himself. There is Isaac, faithful Isaac the Armenian. His appearance needs no complements, for he is Eastern to the eyes—penetrating, dreamy, and narrow.

The two hundred soldiers are all Indians. They are armed to the teeth and wear the discipline of their trade easily, for they are troops from the imperial barracks. Abdullah has connections. Thousands would be at his beck and call, if he wished them. Or more exactly, if they were useful. The Grand Mogul himself has made the Abdullah's safety a personal responsibility, partly in gratitude, partly in policy.

For Abdullah is shaping history. Rather he is about to determine what shape history has taken. A gulf of three centuries lay between the Indias and China. In this dark, mysterious hollow, cries from the thirteenth century echo and re-echo, then drift down Himalayan valleys into imperial and ecclesiastical chambers. Ghosts of the Polos, first roving reporters of these forbidding regions.

In his turban the Abdullah has stuffed letters from the Archbishop of Goa, commendatory letters to kings and vassals of Akbar, and a list of the Church-movable feasts for the next seventeen years. He plucks them forth now for a final assurance that all is in order, and his eyes strain in the misty dawn to discover their contents. Replacing them, he resumes his watch with an impatient sigh. He wonders how long it will be, though his speculations are futile because a torch flares across the waters. The Abdullah mounts his horse. His Kashgar-caravan squeaks and complains into line and rolls away. Into the west. Into an endless passage of rivers, ridges, and valleys.

In 1581 the road from Lahore to Kabul had been measured by Akbar's surveyors. Akbar himself had been on hand, quite by chance, for the surveying turned out to be a by-project during a military campaign to Kabul.

Bringing to their task little besides consummate patience, slaves, or surveyors so-called, turned bamboo poles end for end and month after month while royal officials made notes and calculated numbers. When they had concluded their labors, they announced the distance to be one hundred and thirty-five cos, about three hundred and sixty miles.

Now, in 1603, twenty-two years after Akbar, Abdullah Isai and his companions follow exactly the same route. The Abdullah does it, conscious that the Jesuit Monserrate has gone before him, with the slaves and officials—a trivial detail, but one that brings him into a feeling of closer intimacy with Jesuits everywhere. He is still on "Jesuit trail," and will be till he reaches Kabul. Beyond that he will be a pioneer.

The first stage is easy, a gradual ascent through pleasant valleys. Along the road villages are strung out like big words in a sentence, with countless little words, or settlements in between. Most of the land, tilled by the plow and warm with the sun, refreshes the caravaneers like a meal. What lies idle oppresses no one. It is gentle. It is nature in her expansive mood.

The inhabitants of these valleys, accustomed to centuries of caravans, scarcely pay attention to them. Only the little folk look up from their farm chores and shyly wave a hand as the arabas, great two-wheeled carts, and lines of camels tied to one another pass by. Grown-ups are too busy with spring plowing and planting. The season is short. They can watch caravans another time.

As mile succeeds mile, the countenance of Mother Nature changes. She scowls now, like an old woman hard and cynical scowling at beggary. A spur of the Hindu Kush extends far enough south to bar traffic's way, and trails coil through its canyons with almost careless abandon. Because of the carts and camels the caravan has to proceed at a laggard's pace, progressing sometimes only three miles a day.

The weather turns bitterly cold. Late spring snows mantle the mountains, and in the wooded glens, where camp is often pitched, winter's icy breath still lingers.

To Benito especially the freezing nights become an increasingly great problem. Cold makes his diary and letter writing by candlelight almost impossible, yet write he must. While others toss and snore in their tent-bunks, he scribbles away with stiffened fingers and hunger gnawing at his innards.

"It is still Lent," he writes, "and we are fasting, taking our meal only at night. Though we have to pay much for it, our fare consists only of a little rice with ghee, some coarse cakes, and some onions; if we can get a little salt fish, we count it as a treat, though it causes thirst. The cold is very severe."

Cold and hunger are little. A heavier cross is hurry's impact on the Jesuit's prayer life. "Owing to the difficulties and the turmoil of the journey, I am unable to observe the regular times and forms of prayer. Hence I say ejaculations, communing with God in my heart and thus I gain strength to bear this cross, which to others may seem heavy, but to me is light and pleasant."

Every advance step is made at point of sword. Robber-nations infest these regions far remote from Akbar's imperial authority. Brother Benito carries his eloquent military passes counter-marked by the king carefully, but they are not worth a camel's grunt. For one thing, come skirmish time, the brigands don't tarry for formal presentations and clearance. For another, neither does Benito. So the Slayer of Hostile King's fine commendatory letters repose in their grandiloquence, and Benito, like his companions, takes to the more significant language called force.

At all costs the goods-of-transport must be protected. Particularly the eatables. Precisely these are the attracting magnets for Ali Babi and all his forty thieves of Kashmir and Turkestan.

103

In the deep narrow valleys pack-trains and wagons roll slowly along while their escort skips upper ridges to shoo away possible denizens of the crags. If these ridges are left unattended, rogues of every kind roll boulders on to victim-trains beneath. Besides delight, the stratagem would afford fabulous returns.

De Goes' armed guards (from the imperial barracks!) have not long to wait for displaying their courage. Shortly after the journey's genesis, while the caravan peacefully winds along a narrow valley, loudly bellowing horsemen suddenly appear in the ravine. Swinging their long sabres, they rush upon the soldiers, who take so vigorously to their heels that it requires several days to collect them. The unprotected merchants follow them into the jungles—there is nothing else to do—and here they remain till the brigands retire. The party reorganizes, but members are still missing, especially soldiers, and the procession finally has to start without them.

That settles the matter. On the first suitable occasion, de Goes promises himself, he will dispense with his brave defenders. Guarding merchant goods is responsibility enough. He can't answer for an army of some one else's soldiers besides.

Just one month after departure, on March twenty-fourth, the caravan sights the ancient market-place of Attock. It skirts the city's crumbling walls, then coasts to a halt near the Indus River, at this point but a bow-shot wide. There it remains for two weeks to take needful repose.

IV

On the eighth of April, Benito struck across the river Indus, little dreaming as he battled against the turbulent waters that he would soon arrive at their very source. He was thinking only of Peshawar, just thirty miles ahead, and the possibility of reaching it before the morrow's sun-down.

Peshawar, fattened on trade, was more than tolerable booty, and the ten thousand outlaws lurking in adjacent mountains, particularly in the Khyber Pass just beyond, kept a wary eye for possible indiscretions of the city defenders. Guards had to be posted every night. It was common knowledge along the trail that Peshawar admitted no one, whatever his distinction, after sun-down. To camp just outside the walls was unthinkable—one became suspect, if not stripped. There was no alternative but to plan one's journey accordingly.

Benito reached the fortress just before the dead-line. There was little time to spare after his long caravan had briskly passed through the gates.

In the city they spent a pleasant night. As its citizens were not notably hostile to the Christian Abdullah, he had his moments of peace. There was no news of Cathay, and this was disappointing, for Peshawar's bazaar was the eye and ear of the whole northwest frontier.

On the following morning, the caravan made another start, this time for Jamrud eleven miles distant. The topography of the country became wilder. Its people were wilder. They were mountain-men with the violent prejudices and allegiances of those who absorb some of the fierceness of their surroundings. Among them Benito, with his Christian alias, "Abdullah Isai," met his first opposition.

He was in the market-place at Jamrud, inquiring casually about "lost Christians," scarcely noticing two eavesdroppers who spat indignantly every time the Abdullah said "Christian." They were local toughs, henchmen of a Kashmir rajah whose domain extended south and west to this irregular point. One was obviously the brains of the team, the other the brawn, so between the two of them they made one hefty scoundrel. The husky one, engrossed in his own blind vituperation of the concept "Christian," could never have thought of hailing the Abdullah before his master. That was the role the Brain would have to fill.

And the Brain, had he lived elsewhere or in another time, would have been a robber chief or a dumpy mob king. Here and now he supported the law instead, but his violence, prompted by a rabid xenophobia, was as criminal as any robbery. If he was mean enough to molest any stranger he could catch, he was certainly mean enough to molest the Christian Abdullah. He quickly proposed what the other seized upon, punishment for the Christian dog who had the effrontery to invade Islamism.

The Brain sidled up to the Abdullah.

"You are a Christian dog?" he asked in a mocking tone which he reserved for foreigners and morons.

"I am a Christian." Benito looked from one to the other. "If you are officials," he said, "I have my papers right here."

"I'll take them," said the Brain, snatching at them rudely. "You come with us to the rajah."

"But I have business. . . ."

"Your business will keep."

Some hours later Benito found himself in the presence of a benevolent tyrant who posed as Asia's appeasement for Allah. He took great pride in his orthodoxy.

"You are a Christian mullah?" the rajah asked, rippling serenely.

"I am a Christian," said Benito.

"Then renounce your law and salute the Prophet." The rajah creamed his words and served them slowly.

"My law is my life. One does not lightly dispose of life."

"Will you lose your life then?" The creaming had failed. There was a suggestion of tartness in the rajah's tone. One knee was rocking now, a mannerism that indicated the rajah's irritation. He was nearing the crater of violence.

"I am Your Excellency's humble servant," was Benito's imperturbable reply. "I am also the servant of Jesus Christ who died to save all men. If die I must. . . ." Benito shrugged.

The smile on his face confirmed his interior composure and the discomfited rajah could shake neither Benito's obstinacy nor his great good cheer. Threats only sharpened the Jesuit's wit.

"This Christian dog must die!" roared the rajah, when his meager fund of patience had been exhausted. "Tie him up and drive elephants over his heart!"

"Sire," Benito graciously bowed, "you do me a favor. Gladly I die for the one true God."

He was bustled off to the dungeons till elephants could be readied for their gory task.

Such audacity was unknown even among these fierce mountain-men. "We cannot let him die," the court-officials told one another. "He is too brave." And others

107

added that it was a pity such a brave man would have to go to hell because he wouldn't salute the Prophet.

The rajah, too, had been disarmed by this display of courage. He was moody in his affairs this morning, and he constantly bothered attendants by asking for advice.

"Let him escape," they said, "and thus you will save face." They couldn't understand why such a trifling matter depressed him so.

"No," decided the rajah after a painful struggle with conscience, "I will pay tribute to his great heart by giving him life."

And Benito, quite alive, rejoined the mourning Isaac.

Several days later, while the party was on its way to a small village off the trail, Benito chanced upon a wandering hermit, a ne'er-do-well who scavengered the Khyber Pass approach. Behind his tangled and hoary beard he appeared to be a dwarf or little old elf, all dried up and hardened like the landscape. He wheezed as he talked, but this had little effect on his flow of chatter.

Did the hermit know of Cathay, a community of Christians living apart? No, he didn't, but thirty days' march to the northeast there was the territory called Kafiristan. Its inhabitants were the Siah Posh, so-named because they wore black garments when they worshiped in their temples.

Great Caesar! thought Benito to himself. Siah Posh . . . black garments. The Siah Posh in Lahore were Jesuits!

Did these people have priests without wives and the Mass with bread and wine? No, there was no Mass. But wine—ah! Wine was outlawed (at least theoretically) by the Mohammedans, but among the Siah Posh it was the very song of life! Delightful!

And the hermit produced a sample with which he regaled the thirsty Benito.

Yes, Benito decided, it was good, very much like the wine of his native Villa Franca de Campo in the Azores.

Had the hermit visited this land of the Siah Posh? Oh, many times. It was hill-country and because of this the people had maintained their independence for centuries. Mohammedans hated them as wine-bibbers and called them Kafirs.

The garrulous old hermit babbled away. It wasn't often he had such a good listener; most travellers drove him off like a dog. And Benito soaked in the gossip. He would write it all in his diary just before bed-time.

The Kafirs, the hermit said, had a great regard for their own courage. Not idly so, for it was commonly held that one Kafir was worth five Mohammedans in any battle. Kafirs hated Mohammedans on the basis of race rather than religion, and by tribal custom each went bare-headed till he had slain one of the opposition. To qualify for marriage, he must needs have slain two, and, the hermit added waggishly, there was no dearth of weddings due to corpse default. No one like a Kafir for throat-cutting! And he winked with pleasure.

Had the hermit attended prayer-service or funerals? No, but he had heard that wine was served freely at funerals. A sort of wake. As for religion itself, there were a few natives who professed the prayer of the Prophet. They were not molested. Only foreign Mohammedans were forbidden entrance to the country. So far as he knew, Buddhist or heathen merchants came and went without interference, but they were barred from the temples.

Benito had another sip of wine and the hermit reluctantly bade him good-day.

Three miles beyond Jamrud came the climax of the route between Lahore and Kabul. Also the climax of the route between Asia and Europe, and as such, one of the most important strategic passes in the whole world. It was the Khyber Pass.

Kipling has immortalized it in a swinging ballad, reflecting the mood of all Minor Asia.

> When springtime flushes the desert grass,
> our kafilas wind through the Khyber Pass.
> Lean are the camels but fat the frails,
> Light are the purses but heavy the bales,
> as the snowbound trade of the North comes down
> To the market-square Peshawar town.

For de Goes, the Pass represented more than a geographical climax. It was a gateway, both remote and far, but still a gateway to Europe. Europe's tales and adventures were tied in with it. Europe counted it as the door to the Indian sub-continent, just as India counted it as the last home-defense.

It was a narrow ravine in the southwest-northeast Safed Koh range which served as a wall and water-divide between the Peshawar plains and the Afghan mile-high plateau. At its narrowest point it was only fifteen feet wide, where it could be defended against thousands by a mere handful of soldiers. Nearly everything favored defense: the desert-approach, the cliff-banks above, shale and limestone towering two-thousand feet higher, the plateau where reinforcements could gather.

Many times had a hostile fist rapped at India's door. That door was a secure one—the foe would have to gain entrance through another.

110

Entering the pass, Benito found a trail leading through a barren, stony plain for about three miles. Then it plunged into steeper mountains, ascending along the left side of the ravine to a plateau. Still going west, it zigzagged to the river and followed a cliff-bank, the narrowest point. Three miles farther on, the ravine widened and here there were a few villages of natives called "Pathans" scattered across the mountain meadows. This was a renowned center of Buddhism.

Another plateau seven miles long brought Benito to Landi Kotal, overlooking the truculent plains of Afghanistan. Hidden in its desert-grass were the two centers of trade which must yet be achieved before Kabul.

First there was Jelalabad. It was in a deep basin, covered with sugar cane plantations and almost surrounded by heights of several thousands of feet. During the day these rocky heights absorbed the sun's heat, and at night they gave it out, nearly suffocating native and foreigner alike.

If this were not enough, Jelalabad's sandflies swarmed everywhere. They filled tents and beds and hopped all over their victims and sucked blood till dawn. It was de Goes' joke that his Christian blood had converted half the inhabitants of Jelalabad, a prodigy never admitted by his Mohammedan companions.

Jagdaluk came next, forty dusty miles further on. It consisted mostly of a grove of mulberry trees and a fort where Afghan monarchs in times past had rested from their journeys. For de Goes it held special memories. Robbers near there had been particularly bothersome.

Benito's last sixty miles to Kabul were notably rough. The road struggled north through gorges cut deep in the rugged mountains. Caravan traffic was heavy, going both ways. Afghans were shifting north for the cooler summer. They carried little with them, except their very aged and very young on their camels. Men plodded beside their beasts, and women followed after as best they could. These were the people who, some generations later, would annihilate the British in these same gorges, sparing only one man to tell the tale.

Moving south were Kabul's products, vast herds of horses, dyes, gold-thread, Afghan carpets and silks, and, above all, wool clipped twice yearly from the flocks of the cold north. There was drama in the swinging gait of the pack-animals. The drama of trade. The drama of get-rich-quick or get-murdered-and-lose-all.

Since all roads have to end sooner or later, Benito's, too, at last ran out. Early summer had come when his caravan rolled wearily through the Kabul Valley. Promise was in the valley air, fruits swelling in orchards, herbs springing and stretching from the earth. Ewes were nursing lambs; and mares, their colts. Isolated by its fierce mountains and deserts, the valley was a friendly, smiling island of plenty, doubly welcome to the wayfarer.

For Abdullah Isai it was the end of one trail and the beginning of another.

V

In Kabul the Kashgar-caravan disbanded. Though business beckoned the merchants farther along the trail, not many would heed its call. They had been dismayed by the dangers and hardships of their journey. They preferred to return home, to recover their health and retire, if possible, on the fortunes accumulated from past risks. With all hurry and dispatch they traded goods

112

brought hence for Kabul's dyes, silks, and woolens, and reloaded their beasts for the drop on to the hot plains of India.

They wanted the Abdullah to return with them. "Get off the trails before winter sets in," they said, "or you will surely perish in a blizzard."

To return would have suited de Goes just right, but there was no turning back now. With Spartan indifference he began his preparations for the next stage.

He first discharged his stout imperial escort, not without celebrations by those concerned, and accepted the resignations of Demetrius and Grimon. The former discovered new possibilities of money-making in Kabul and begged to be excused. The latter, Christian and holy sub-deacon, had heart only for his wife at home. He must go back to the family, he said, and Benito agreed while he wrily considered the Church's wisdom in its celibate clergy.

Only Isaac, faithful Isaac the Armenian, was left. This much, at least, was fortunate, for between Benito and Isaac a bond of affection had sprung. To the very end Isaac was purse, staff, and girdle for the Jesuit Brother.

In Kabul, Benito and Isaac, like stray dogs on forage, wandered from bazaar to bazaar searching for scraps of geographical gossip. "Ever hear of Cathay?" they asked. "Have you heard of a Christian city called Cambuluc?" They often crossed paths with local characters and summarily pumped them for what they were worth.

In the course of these wanderings, Benito chanced upon a Princess in distress, a real, live princess. He called her "Hajji-Khanem," meaning princess-pilgrim. She was most charming. She was pious, too, and as she peeped over the top of her veil, wondrously beautiful. The years had spared her, for already there were some who could call her "Grandma." Her son was the lord and high mighty of Khotan, jade-rich kingdom east of Turkestan.

It would seem that Hajji-Khanem was returning from Mecca where she had paid her respects at the tomb of the Prophet. Coming through the mountain passes, her party had been pounced upon by those playboys of the boulders and stripped of all goods. Now here she was in Kabul, grateful for life, but in a state of utter destitution. Her countrymen had coldly turned her appeals aside. Would the Christian Abdullah lend her, at generous interest, to be sure, the funds she needed?

Benito, like the robbers, cannily pounced upon the opportunity. Plainly here was a lady worth knowing. Mother of a king. Sister of another king. What gates through Central Asia would this gallantry swing wide? What bribes would it spare him? Indeed! The Abdullah was most willing.

He feverishly sold part of his merchandise, then hastened to the princess-pilgrim.

"Here," he said, "are six hundred gold pieces. Take them. They are yours."

Only one demand did he make of her. The sum was to be returned to him in the form of "transparent marble," which was jade.

Of course the Princess was delighted and she embarrassed the shy Jesuit with her say-so.

"Allah has sent you to me! May Allah reward you! Allah be praised!"

"Amen," said Benito. Mumbling his polite good-byes, he left the field to Isaac. The trail ahead was more important.

If Benito had counted among his means of transport a Magic Carpet (or better yet, a sky-clipper), he could have made the hop from Kabul to Teshkan in two hours of any Arabian day or night. As it was, the journey took the better part of two months.

And, of course, Benito was spared none of the wretched villages enroute, which is to say, none of the refined annoyances of Asian travel. First there was in all villages the special problem of women. Caravaneers were allowed, even expected, to take temporary "wives" during stop-over periods in cities or villages. Hosts obligingly turned over their own wives or daughters for the travellers' convenience; and if their "courtesy" was not accepted, enemies were made, and threats as well, and a hue and cry went up that customs were being violated. Law-abiding folk condemned before their very eyes! Obviously Benito could have nothing to do with such a vicious practice. He had taken a vow of perpetual chastity and he was determined to keep it no matter what the cost to him. Far better was life in the open where threats could be energetically resisted. A cobra or a lion was less dangerous and easier to drive off than a thousand irate liberals who considered themselves insulted by a foreign devil called Abdullah Isai.

Next, there was that pestilence in all villages, the ubiquitous toll-collector. On this rim of Akbar's dominions, royal letters of tax-exemption were scorned as much by officials as passports had heretofore been by outlaws. In every village there was the same old struggle, with the Christian Abdullah shouting the same old arguments.

One can see the pattern. Tax-gatherers smile expectantly as the pretentious Abdullah approaches. They read his testimonials. Their smiles vanish and they bark at him to pay up. Or else. Of what use are the Grand Mogul's boasts in this remote province? Slayer of Hostile Kings—indeed! He will slay no one. The Abdullah bargains, haggles like a native with whom it is a game. Nothing restores immunity. He reluctantly fishes for his purse.

If that were not enough, there were always local mosque taxes, too, and fines for not appearing at prayer service on Holy Days. No measure of expostulating won exemption from mullahs dependent on fines for "the better life." And so many mullahs. The purse again, of course, or there was neither rest nor escape.

Small wonder it is, then, that de Goes found every city and village "disappointing." They were much worse. They were men-traps where a man wasn't so much fleeced as bled.

As for the trail, it was a haunted one, and its ghost was no less than Alexander of Macedonia. This was his country, the land he gave his life to conquer. De Goes found his foot-prints everywhere. Also his celebrated horse, because every single native of that vast empire boasted that his mount was the one and only descendant of Bucephalus. That there were a million such descendants counted for nothing, because each saw only his own.

On the other hand, despite the distinguished ghost and horses, there were no Christians. When Benito finally arrived in Charikar, there were not even rumors of Christians. There were only the Prophet's fanatics and iron, both in abundance.

The iron lay buried in neighboring mountains. It was a generous deposit (whole ranges of it) and locals took great pride in it as if they had put it there. When Benito made inquiries, for the sake of his journal rather than investment, he was referred to a hamlet buried like the iron, where one could examine at leisure. Benito took the side-trip.

116

Several hours after his arrival there, he had a new friend, a life-long friend if by that is meant a staunch one. He was almost a caricature, this friend, bloated and hoarse like a bullfrog. His eyes, which were the most prominent features of the head, protruded significantly, and their lids hung half-way, toad-like, suggesting a drowsy interior. To look at him in his muddy-green frock, one expected to find telltale warts. Instead, his coat stuck to him as smooth as sausage skin, with not a wrinkle to spare.

Ben Ali was a monument in the village. He possessed a generous measure of dry wit and could amicably solve disputes among the battle lusty and could philosophize agreeably on life's tribulations or the hardships of love. That he did not rank as a chief should be attributed to his need for enterprise. He was neither forceful nor ambitious and that was his life-guarantee. For the cruel, who usually rule in a crude society, could find no reason whatever for liquidating this delightful frog.

Ben Ali had lots to say, mostly about iron and the local lion hunt, excellent if one sought the right jungles and had goats enough for bait. Nothing would have suited the old fellow more than a big-scale hunt with the Abdullah footing the bills and Ben Ali claiming the trophies. But de Goes, despite his desire to humor him, would not hear of it. Instead of taking to the hills, he announced his return to Charikar and began the elaborate Oriental farewell.

During the same, Ben Ali was grief-struck. He had almost come to believe Benito would be a patron for his wit. Amidst tears and exclamations to Allah, Benito left; and before he was gone an hour, the frog was croaking as gaily as ever.

Parwan was another goal, like the inch on a yardstick.

117

Somewhere between end and end. "A small but busy town," was de Goes' laconic comment, referring, perhaps, to the lucrative stopover service which it provided for caravans like Benito's. It stayed in Parwan for five tedious days, theoretically for a rest before attempting a difficult pass just ahead.

It was called the Parwan Pass and it had seven smaller ones leading up to it—a sort of stairway built on Paul Bunyan scale with God's own granite. It commanded the Hindu Kush and trail on to the "Roof of the World," both of which were high altitude areas with few equals in the world. The former was an approach for the latter and a kind of testing ground for one's courage to proceed.

It took de Goes twenty days to cross this course with its preliminaries. Fifteen more days of ascent and descent brought him to the land of the Calcias who, so their name implied, were hard put for a place to hang their goat-hair turbans. In their language Calcia meant "forced to retire into the mountains in order to live." They were fair-haired and blue-eyed, like the Flemish, and they carried stiff, scraggly beards of reddish-brown and swung a mean arm in battle.

In that summer of 1603 they were in revolt against the regional khan. Finding him elusive, or more often, barricaded behind his Samarkand walls, they took their vengeance out on any travellers they could catch. And that was quite an order.

De Goes and companions ran their gauntlet without mishap, though lions kept them on the alert when Calcias didn't. It was in these mountains that Alexander (according to Quintus Curtius) killed an enormous lion, and Benito's party killed a few too. There was no Quintus to record them, so the number is left to posterity's conjecture. No one dared go after water alone, for nearly every watering-hole had its ferocious sentinel, waiting for a mutton dinner, but only too eager to substitute a plump Abdullah, with or without seasoning.

After the Calcias and lions came Talikan, in some ways worse than either. Whether one reached it by Magic Carpet or trail, it, too, was "disappointing." Just a wretched village of several hundred huts, swarming with beggars. Civil war had reduced it to this indecency from the imposing city Marco Polo had found on his arrival. "A flourishing corn market with mountains of salt," reported Marco of Talikan. The salt was still there, in supplies vast enough to salt all Turkestan, and small expeditions arrived daily to gather the mineral for cooking.

From these expeditionaries Benito made inquiries about all the land of the region. No Christians. Just more descendants of Bucephalus, and, what is perhaps more astonishing, descendants of Alexander himself. Hundreds of them, all "genuine." Not too far away lay the world-famous Balas ruby mines, carefully guarded by the king's agents and exploited with canny royal providence.

To the northwest, the salt-diggers said, was Samarkand, once capital of the great Tamerlane, Akbar's forbear. There, covered by a mosque of his own execution, his bones still rested in an ivory coffin. And over his tomb in Arabic-Alabaster letters were the words, "Were I still alive mankind would tremble." Tamerlane, they added, was still alive in the persons of their tyrants.

Mankind indeed did tremble, including these poor peasants who needed but peace and salt in their stew to be happy.

119

The natives of Talikan, clad in their sheep-skin jackets and boots home-made of the same stuff, sat around in wine shops eating their favorite beverage instead of drinking it. For boiled wine, in the consistency of jelly, was much in vogue and no one would do without it, not even for man-killing, which played a good second as Talikan's pastime. The ruined city was evidence enough for that.

After several weeks in this wretched hole, the caravan shoved off again for the fortress of Teshkan. The distance to the latter was not so long. Neither was the trail so wide. In some places, in fact, it was so narrow that Benito kept wondering if it had been made for spirits. To get a packhorse over these narrow ledges was a feat of no mean proportions. First the beast was relieved of its burden, usually one hundred and twenty pounds, then with a couple of strong men pulling on the halter and two or three more hanging on the tail, the quivering animal was slowly maneuvered across. Sometimes it happened that horse and horse-pullers plunged into the abyss. They would turn somersaults in mid-air and disappear forever. Whether this happened or not, the possibility remained as presage of the future. There was worse to come.

Near Teshkan, Benito's caravan encamped for brief respite. At once, even before campfires were kindled, a messenger appeared from the town. The governor of Samarkand, he said, insisted that the caravan hasten within protecting city walls. Hordes of Tartars were devastating the country and he, the royal and supreme governor (though he didn't like to press the point), feared the more lest these scoundrels attack the caravan and lead away badly needed horses.

Into the town the weary merchants betook themselves,

120

but to their dismay they found more thieves within than without. They soon abandoned the den, and the governor, like a possessive rooster, strutted after them with numerous guards. It was his duty, he loudly crowed, to prevent the devilish Tartars from getting horses. For this, as any brave man, he would die. But alas! Scarcely had all cleared the city walls when on the horizon appeared—yes, Tartars! The plucky governor and his less assertive soldiers scattered like rabbits.

"We'll fight," yelled Benito.

There was nothing else to do. Bales were piled into barricades; flint rocks were scraped together for ammunition should the arrows give out.

When the Tartars arrived on the spot, they decided to stall. Here was their booty. What need for haste? They sent forward envoys of peace who indulged pompously in meaningless double-talk. But no one was impressed by this Tartar benevolence. As soon as the messengers made off, the merchants determined to take advantage of the truce by retreating. Leaving their bales, they scrambled into the nearest woods and from behind their trees watched the robbers tranquilly approach and dive into bags of treasure. They were like rowdy kids in a warehouse. The quantity and sparkle cast a spell over them and, as they robbed and pillaged, they whistled and danced.

Then their master arrived, the chief of the tribe. He forced all of his men to put back what they had taken, called for the merchants, and helped them reorganize their caravan.

For these proceedings the Tartars had little taste. They split into bands and followed on the heels of the caravan to harass and nag stragglers. Several days later, as Benito lagged behind to attend to his prayers, four of

121

these rascals ambushed him and like the tigers, which frequented that area, crouched for the spring. Benito spotted them just in time. Quickly he tore off his turban, flung it as far as he could, and set spurs to his horse. While the hunters quarrelled over this glittering bait, Benito was away.

Akbar's jewels were gone, the jewels that he had contributed for Benito's fine turban. And the robber who had them? He would probably sell them to the first caravan going south. Perhaps they would turn up at Lahore, Benito thought, chuckling to himself at what consternation this would occasion.

VI

While the traveller crossed the cultivated plains of Badakshan, through fields of huskless barley and groves of walnut, only one thought filled his mind: the "Roof of the World," which lay ahead.

The roof of the world it was. A mysterious, silent wasteland of ice and snow and rock, shrouded in a perpetual mist, encompassed by the noblest mountains on earth. It was not so much a plateau as a series of six peak-high levels of filled-in glacial wash, once valleys, now tables as lofty as Europe's Mont Blanc. These formed a kind of pivot point for the four great mountain ranges of Central Asia, not the least of which was the Himalayan. All around rose great clusters of ice-cones, awesome in their splendor like fantastic heights for a fairy-tale castle. The highest altitudes on earth. Legend peopled them with mortals who were immortal. Indians almost worshiped them, and the Chinese, whose lands bordered on the north, counted them as the half-way point between the sea and the heavens and they feared their power as much as they jealously guarded their portion through the centuries.

Marco Polo had crossed the "Roof of the World" in the thirteenth century and he called the several high levels "Pamirs," which meant "an uninhabitable country which has inhabitants." Pamirs varied in length and width—the smallest, Little Pamir, was sixty-eight miles long—but they had certain features in common. All were bleak and boulder-strewn. All met the sky and merged into it almost without lineament, like grey merging into pale blue. All presented the same hazards to animal life: rarefied atmosphere, high winds, severe colds, and blizzards.

Whether the traveller took this or that Pamir to connect with the China trail, he had to face mountain-sickness occasioned by the great altitude. It was a curse not unlike sea-sickness, with tribute paid in other coin. Headaches were extreme; nausea, ear-buzzing, bleeding lungs, and quickened pulse were the common reactions. Sleep came reluctantly, appetite not at all. Men and animals died with equal disinterest. Those who survived sickened even more with the means of survival, dried apples, onions, and garlic. For such were the grim remedies prescribed.

Garlic in abundance was strapped to horses' backs and periodically halts were made to rub it into festering gums. This, de Goes was told, retarded circulation and so prolonged animal energies. Whether it was efficacious or not no one questioned, just as no one questioned whether bleeding was good for "fever." It was always done. Who could afford to take chances?

The lowly garlic was guarded as carefully as life itself.

As was customary, native guides were hired to lead

123

Benito's caravan across the "Roof of the World." They were three in number and Kirghiz in race. Their people were hardy nomads who pastured their flocks in the Pamirs during the summer months. When autumn came, they slipped down into warmer valleys and managed somehow to survive the winters by keeping to their yurts.

Like the wolves, the Kirghiz depended on the country's wild sheep, huge beasts with horns that measured more than five feet from tip to tip. Sheepskins were the Kirghiz garments, mutton and sour milk their steady diet. Sheep horns served as fences for corrals; with trimmed sheep horns they shod their horses, protesting vigorously that, so shod, a horse could go any-where a sheep could go.

Their contention was an honest one, as the caravaneers would soon discover. The wiry, well-shod ponies of the Kirghiz could leave the caravan's best horse-flesh far behind, at least on Kirghiz ground, on the "Roof of the World."

Fortunately the three guides obtained were the best, simple and honest, yet almost uncanny in detecting dangers for the caravan. They could talk a little Persian, a feat which set them apart among their tribesmen, who scarcely bothered to learn their own tongue. The silence of high altitudes had seeped into their very bones and left them silent men, inscrutable men.

Kirghiz as a rule were not much interested in the out-side world. They knew too little about it. But guides, who enjoyed some contact, were often very inquisitive. They asked innumerable questions, explored every man's personality, taking nothing at all for granted, not even a man's looks. If he had big ears or a wart on his nose, they asked about it.

124

Some of the caravaneers resented this curiosity as an intrusion, Isaac more than the others; so he especially relished Benito's first encounter with the Kirghiz race.

"Ho! there, boy; that your horse?"

Isaac was brushing down Pegasus with cautious, affectionate strokes. He turned up to see one of the Kirghiz guides goggling enviously. Isaac's face flushed with pleasure—he shared Benito's great pride in the animal. "No," he said, turning back to his brushing, "not my horse. It's my master's horse."

Benito had got Pegasus as a gift from the merchant John Galiseo, Father Emmanuel's friend. It was a beauty, a shimmering chestnut with white markings on its face and fore-legs.

"That your dog?" said the guide.

Isaac looked up again. "Yes, that's my dog."

The Kirghiz eyed the dog hungrily. Good eating, fat, not too old.

"What's the name of the horse?" he said after a critical pause.

"Pegasus," said Isaac.

"Pegasus?" said the Kirghiz guide. "That's a strange name for a horse. We don't have horses with the name Pegasus." He shook his head and grinned foolishly. When he grinned, his mouth spread almost to the ears and his teeth showed up and down like two saws. For all the world he resembled a good-natured jack-o-lantern. "What does Pegasus mean?" he asked.

"There's my master. Ask him."

"It's the name of a star," said Benito.

"A star?" said the Kirghiz.

"Yes," said Benito, "but that horse there is named after a flying horse, a horse with wings, whose name was Pegasus."

125

"A flying horse?" said the Kirghiz guide, catching on slowly. "But that's impossible. Do horses on the plains have wings?"

"Not all of them," said Benito very soberly.

From behind the horse, Isaac tittered furtively; then suddenly he began to brush the beast with a renewed fervor.

Benito's expedition crossed the "Roof of the World" in early autumn, when snow had already enveloped nature's battlements. Animals that hibernated, marmots for example, had all disappeared. Winds whistled through the corridors like concentrated gales, stirring up great gusts of snowflakes which penetrated the tightest wrappings. Fuel for fire was almost impossible to find. A few argols, dried camel or yak dung, were gathered up along the way, but they were damp and smoked more than they burned.

For forty days and nights the caravaneers battled mountain-sickness, blizzards, bandits, and wolves on the "Roof of the World." No one dared to be alone. Horses and supplies had to be guarded every second. Five of Benito's horses died from exhaustion and cold. He had difficulty keeping the others alive, using more prayers than garlic with favorable results because other merchants lost more than he did.

At night they huddled about their smoking smudges and tried to stave off brooding by telling tales of the hunt and battle and especially of wolves. While they talked, they chewed on dried apples and sipped their tea, which was miserable because water boiled before it was hot enough. At that altitude not even rice could be softened, rice which was their daily food.

The Kirghiz guides liked these fireside gatherings. The weird setting gave them a responsive audience and

126

a chance to ask questions too. At first they talked much about robbers on the "Roof of the World." The world's worst, one of them said. Robbers banished from all respectable robber-bands, another one added. But mostly the Kirghiz talked about their hereditary enemies, the wolves. The wolves' thirst for blood was unquenchable, they said. Wolves killed sheep and Kirghiz just for revenge. The wolf was an evil demon.

"But let the wolf beware!" cried one of the Kirghiz loyally. "When we catch him, we put blocks of wood between his jaws and we bind thongs about the blocks. Then we put dry snuff into his snout and turn him loose and torture him with whips and hot coals. When we get good and ready, we put his eyes out. And then we kill him."

All the Kirghiz grunted their approval. "That for the wolf," they said.

Somebody else talked about horses in the Gobi, horses that could run faster than the wind. Like sheep they could outrun wolves, but in combat they hadn't a chance. At watering holes where all the animals of the desert met, wolves tore into herds like demons—the horses hadn't a chance. A great pity it was.

The Gobi? said another. He had hunted camels on the Gobi with a Buddhist. They got lost and were dying of starvation. Then they espied some ducks nesting on a little slough. With Allah's help he caught one and was going to wring its neck—by his beard! He was hungry for that duck! But the Buddhist stopped him. He said that ducks were lamas among birds, that it was a crime to kill one because it might be the reincarnation of Buddha.

Then a Kirghiz guide looked at Benito, who was listening intently.

"The Christian Abdullah," he said, still grinning like a jack-o-lantern, "has a flying horse. Perhaps the Christian Abdullah would tell us about his horse that flies."

"About Pegasus?" said Benito, alert to the mischief there. "I'll tell you about all flying horses, all of them with the name Pegasus.

"Once upon a time," he began and paused dramatically, he was sure that his audience wanted acting with the story, "in the far away land of ancient Greece, there were three sisters. They were ugly as toads and their hair was like snakes and anyone who looked upon them was turned into stone."

A shiver of terror swept through his listeners.

"One of these sisters had the name Medusa. She was ugliest of all; she was as ugly as a *horned* toad.

"Now there was a great hero among the Greeks called Perseus, and Perseus was determined to kill all the ugly sisters. So he got himself a bright shield and he polished it till it shone like the sun. Then he went hunting for Medusa. When he came to her lodging, he didn't look at her, but he held his shield up and he saw her reflection, and in this way he killed her. He cut off her head. And when she died, her spirit turned into a winged horse which flew off to the holy mountains.

"That horse's name was Pegasus and all winged horses go by the name of Pegasus. My horse goes up into the sky, over the 'Roof of the World,' so it is Pegasus too. And that's the end."

"Did those flying horses eat garlic, like yours?" asked the grinning guide incredulously, betraying his suspicion that it might possibly not be true.

"No," said Benito solemnly, "they lived on the odor of it."

Everyone laughed. The Abdullah was a good fellow, they said, even if he was an infidel Christian.

128

After the first week had passed, the trail ran into a mountain so steep that only the strongest horses could climb it. Then it dipped into a valley where the earth was rounded and green, and a few twigs were found for fuel. Marmots, sitting on their haunches, whistled sharp warnings to their neighbors, and even the horses showed their pleasure at this new sign of life.

In the distance a faint, wispy coil of smoke could be seen, issuing from a yurt and fading away in the thin-bluish sky. The merchants made haste, for they were sure of a welcome.

Three yurts there were, just a small camp of a patriarch with his clan, late-leavers of the pasture grounds above. Wool-heavy flocks grazed peacefully round about and in their midst was the patriarch with all his family, his children, in-laws, and grand-children. One tiny lad, clad in a sheepskin cap with great fur flaps and his father's huge boots, peeked shyly from behind his mother and his eyes were as wide as cups. The women had no veils, which was quite a marvel in itself. They differed mostly from Western women by their slit-eyes and white calico turbans wound like a hornet's nest on their heads.

The Kirghiz were most pleasant. Benito made friends with them in a moment, although he had to use a guide as interpreter. They showed him their yurts which were tents of felt, cylindrical at the base and hemispheric at the top, and mounted on wheels. Near by stood the motive power, yaks stolidly chewing their cuds and gazing off into space, as if today were no different from any other day.

They were strange beasts, partakers of qualities of three or more other animals, the buffalo, the ox, and the camel. What the wild sheep didn't supply for the

Kirghiz, the yaks did. Milk to drink. Horns to drink out of. Flesh to eat. Its dung was fuel and its tail a good fly-whisk. It could carry a pack or pull a cart, and when needed badly enough, could serve as a saddle-horse. Its legs were too short for speed, but what it lacked in quality, it made up in quantity.

Life for the Kirghiz was hard in the extreme. To be weak was to court death. To yield was to be cast aside. Constant warfare with the elements and animals had sharpened their ingenuity, and, as one might suspect, they lived to an incredibly ripe age. The patriarch of this clan was over ninety. When Benito expressed surprise at his heartiness, he was told of a neighbor, a man one hundred and ten years old, who, when he came to visit, brought his five sons with him, all over seventy and graced with long, hoary beards.

Benito asked about the struggle between wolves and wild-sheep.

"Wolves!" snarled the old patriarch, bitter with memories. "The sheep have no chance. No," he wagged his head sadly, "not even a chance with their fine horns. They can only run, but seldom escape. Even when they leap over cliffs—and they land safely on their horns—wolves are at the bottom, waiting to make a feast of them. And we are like sheep . . . we cannot stray. . . ."

A tragedy, perhaps several, lurked in his solemn tones.

After leaving the Kirghiz, the caravan spent five days in the open in torrential rains. They had no fires and almost no food, but they couldn't turn back. They hurried forward to outrun famine which seemed, like the wolf, always to nip at their heels. Ten days of this: then they reached the country of Sarikol. What they expected is difficult to say, but they found little. Two

130

precious days were taken to revive their jaded horses and after that it was the trail again, their killing pace.

Now it was climbing that tried their endurance. Just ahead was Wakhjir Pass, reputed to be the most difficult enroute. It was 16,150 feet high and could be approached only by paths scarcely wide enough for horses. To the left towered unrelenting stone. To the right were precipitate river-canyons, the bottoms of which were lost in haze. One knew there was a bottom only when a companion slipped into the abyss; then shrieks of a tumbling human being echoed against that other world, assuring all of bottoms and unburied bones.

In breathless moments the Mohammedans called upon their Prophet to help them. "May Allah help me!" they gasped. "May Allah help me!" And after the passage had been successfully crossed, they fell on their knees to thank Allah.

From the summit of Wakhjir other peaks extended four thousand feet higher. In silence and solitude they brooded over that vast world, a seeming chaos in a God-forsaken wasteland.

The caravan snaked along the icy slopes in single file, not a little frightened by the terrible silence. On the eastern horizon they could see another pass, Chichiklik, stretching like a challenge across the skyline. It was only nine miles away, but thousands in terms of effort.

The trail dropped into a valley of death. Six more horses rolled over and died, but human beings managed to survive. And the end was not yet. Far from it.

Chichiklik was a gap more lofty than the highest mountain in the United States and as high as two Rocky Mountain passes piled on one another. Along its crown lay snow twenty feet deep, and for six days the caravan had to plow through it. Several merchants perished from the cold. Avalanches buried others. Brother de Goes himself became gravely ill with fever and barely escaped the relentless Pursuer Death.

Downward the trail became increasingly worse. For the most part now it was a river bed at the base of a deep canyon. Besides the dark, foreboding walls of the canyon, only a narrow ribbon of blue shone above. The roar of turbulent waters echoing and re-echoing in this sound-prison was deafening. Deep pools interspersed the more shallow waters, so horses had to proceed very cautiously. Before taking a step they had to feel for footing and often enough lost their balance entirely. At other times they were forced to leap from boulder to boulder, an evolution about as natural to them as cantering for a goat. Five more of the shrinking herd perished and were washed away.

To climax Benito's anguish, faithful Isaac plunged from a cliff into icy waters below. Benito dived after him and finally dragged him on to a ledge. For eight hours he prayed and rubbed while all but himself despaired. "He is a dead man," they said. "Save your strength." But Isaac was not dead. He recovered and took again to the miserable path.

After a fifteen-day descent, the caravan pulled into a shabby little village. The horrors of famine and cold had left their mark. All but Benito despaired of going one step farther.

"We cannot," the merchants groaned with fires of fever in their eyes.

"Some one must," snapped de Goes, and he began his preparations. He chose the best horse that was left them. He sacked a scant measure of rice and rolled his blankets. At dawn he was off.

For five more terrible days he raced against death, a

132

lone, tragic shadow cast against forces as black as hell. On the fifth evening he sighted the gates of Yarkand, flourishing capital of Turkestan. Diffidently he drew near. Would his papers be accepted? If not, all was lost.

"Your passports," the gatekeeper mumbled in Persian, his hand open not so much for papers as bribes.

Benito produced both and waited. It was like waiting for the surgeon's knife.

"Pass on," said the guard, and he handed Benito his packet.

Benito trotted his horse through the short tunnel. He suddenly felt weak. His strength had vanished.

Ten days later the rest of the party joined Benito at his lodgings. He had sent a rescue expedition to gather them in and all acknowledged his services. He alone, they loudly declared, had saved the caravan.

It was late November, 1603. Benito and Isaac had now been ten months in the mountains. They had completed a journey of 1240 miles, a distance only as long as the Rocky Mountains from Mexico to Canada. The obvious marvel was not the distance negotiated, but the nature of their obstacle-course. Hardly another route in the inhabited world bristled with such opposition. Passes higher than Pike's Peak, gorges as rugged as the Grand Canyon, rivers like the Snake, dens of robbers, hostile religious fanatics, iron curtains, colds and heats of the jungles—all of these in the course of ten months!

VII

Yarkand was a Moslem nest crowded with fanatics and prophets and all manner of bigots. A Christian was about as welcome there as he would be in the Kremlin;

probably less so, for popular as well as official sympathies were against him. Immunity came only from boldness and Benito had to scrape together all he possessed.

Scarcely had he entered the City when his arrival was noised about; a "Giaour," hated Western infidel, was in their very midst! He had walked right in! It was the sensation of the year. Old-timers declared it an unprecedented event, and there were many who said it was too fantastic to be true.

"He is not a Christian," they confidently repeated, just to reassure themselves. "He is a Buddhist who acts like a Christian."

Others cried, "No! He is a Christian!" They raised their voices to consecrate a shaky certitude and their goitres (nearly all citizens of Yarkand were goitred) jerked abruptly to add solemnity to the ceremony. "The king will soon pluck his goose!" they prophesied and with that they looked for the speedy demise of Abdullah Isai.

A name like Abdullah Isai might have dispelled doubts but it was useless for quelling the commotion. The "Armenian Rume," as many locals cynically referred to him, insisted on the "Isai," and this in a manner that brooked no compromise. They quickly learned to allow him his title and all the while wondered about certain perplexities brought on by his arrival.

How was it that the world contained an intelligent man who followed a law besides their own? Anyone could tell you that intelligence demanded submission to the Koran (and no questions asked). Yet here was one who bore a contradiction before them, an obviously intelligent being with the name Abdullah Isai!

Was the Abdullah bewitched? Was truth divided?

134

Surely they thought the Koran was right, whatever the Christian Bible might be.

Their king, it must be said, was as intolerant in religion as the next person. Even more so. He had contrived a delightful procedure for conversion to his own persuasion, horseshoe nails driven into the skulls of dissenters. That few resisted this royal fervor was evident from everyone's reaction to the Abdullah.

And the Abdullah, conscious of the king's brand of Mohammedanism, determined to soften the old bigot in his own fortress. Perhaps it would be like waving a red flag, instead of a white one, but then he would see. He armed himself with his weapons of appeasement and proceeded to the palace.

Abdullah Isai found the king surrounded by an assorted collection of long-beards. He seemed benevolent in appearance, Abdullah said afterwards to Isaac, but suspicious and vengeful as youth.

"Is this the Christian dog who dares to pollute the air of our city?" they whispered to one another. All stretched their necks to examine so rare a freak.

Benito spread his palms toward the ground and inclined his head.

"Your Brilliant Majesty," he began, "I am your humble servant. I have brought your Majesty gifts." He placed a watch, four mirrors, loaves of sugar, and a quantity of candy and fabrics before the king. The cloth was white with colored stripes, and this in itself was wonderful enough.

Benito beamed like a moon over his tribute, pausing long enough to observe repercussions. Then with a nod to the spectators and another bow to the king, he swept out of sight. The long-beards, cautious as cats, watched with open-mouthed wonder. Incredible!

135

Come morning, a royal servant called on the Abdullah. He must inspect the foreign Rume's lodgings, he said, and his sharp eyes searched out all Benito's belongings. They fell upon objects strange for the Mohammedan, a crucifix and Benito's breviary. He demanded them for examination in court.

"No, no," Benito pleaded. "Not these. They are all I have. Please allow me these and say nothing to the king."

So earnest was his begging that the servant professed himself deeply moved. "I promise to say nothing," he said.

And forthwith he sneaked off to the king.

Within the hour Benito was summoned to court.

"Bring the book and all else." The messenger added it vaguely. It was, he knew, a lame effort to describe the unthinkable.

Benito hurried his subversive weapons to the palace, weapons just as subversive in some strangely "Christian" circles across the world.

"This," he said to the king, "is a Roman breviary." He placed it on his head, then kissed it.

"Let me see it," said the king.

Benito put it on his head again, then kissed it. He handed it to an attendant, who caught the fever and also put it on his head and kissed it. Finally it went to the king, who put it on his head and kissed it while all the lords gawked with popping eyes.

"This is small writing," cried the king. "Can anyone read it?"

"Yes, Your Majesty." Benito took the book and opened it at random. He solemnly intoned the first passage that met his eye.

"*Viri Galilaei, quid statis aspicientes in caelum?*" "Ye

136

men of Galilee, why stand you here looking up into heaven?" Then he preached a sermon on the text. So stirred was he as he spoke that tears rolled down his cheeks and all the courtiers wept and sighed with him.

"What marvelous thing is this?" cried the king.

When asked to exhibit the cross, Benito pulled it out and kissed it with great respect. "This," he said, "is the symbol of Christians, and when we pray, we place it before us."

"When you pray, in what direction do you turn?"

"To all directions, for God is in all."

One of the mullahs then inquired if Christians used ablutions.

"Not as Mohammedans do," said Benito. "Our ablutions are spiritual, cleansing the conscience. For we hold that mere outward washings cannot profit the soul while the conscience is full of sin and uncleanness."

"That sounds reasonable," sniffed the king. He was beginning to wonder where his inquisition would end.

All the mullahs muttered ominously in their beards. "Read some more," said a young one whose beard scarcely concealed his goitre.

The Abdullah opened the breviary again and read the Psalm beginning "*Miserere mei Deus.*" He explained this latter to them, dwelling at great length on the Day of Judgment. If, in his first approach, he lacked fire and brimstone, it was because he was saving it for later.

"What marvelous thing is this?" the king kept saying to himself. He had spent his days persecuting unbelievers, and now, for the first time, doubts began to assail him. Had his course been a wise one . . . ?

The king sent for the Jesuit many times. On one occasion he showed him a stack of manuscripts that had come to him with palace possessions when he reached his majority. No one had been able to tell the king what message they bore, so now he pulled several out and asked the Abdullah to read them.

The Abdullah took them into his hands and examined their rich illuminations. The writing was in deep red and there were many abbreviations of words, so he had to read closely.

"These papers concern the mystery of the Holy Trinity," he said at length. He read the Latin words aloud, then spoke on this subject, emphasizing the unity of God, His greatness and omnipotence; how all things that we see depend upon Him, and He on nothing; how He was the beginning and end of all things.

The Abdullah's listeners were greatly impressed again, and they said to one another, "Are these the people we call Christians? Their knowledge of God is no less than ours!"

The king ended the discussion by nodding his head and grunting as though puzzled, "Why, this man is a mullah!"

Not long afterwards the chiefs among the Mohammedans held a meeting.

"How excellent," cried the ringleader, "if we can force this man to accept the law of salvation! For it is grievous to think that one so worthy of respect must die and go to hell!" And he frowned upon all present as though his wife had deserted him and the world lay in ashes at his feet.

"What is the use of talking like this?" asked another. "You may strike him on the head with a sledge-hammer, but do not think you will make him abandon his law."

Some one told Benito about a wager that had been made. A certain most optimistic Mohammedan had bargained that he could force the Abdullah's consent to the Law. He began a petty persecution that lasted day and night, till the evening Benito went to his home.

"Sire," demanded the indignant Benito, "why do you take all this useless trouble? You do not understand that my law is the very core of my being. If it is my property you want, take it. You know where it is. Or here is my body—you can tear it to pieces if you like. In either case," he drew himself up stiffly, "I shall consider myself fortunate."

That was the end of the wager.

But it wasn't the end of Mohammedan maneuvering. The king's chief minister, a very powerful lord by the name of Mirza Ghyas, invited the Abdullah for an evening of discussion. His friends wanted to challenge certain Christian tenets and they preferred to do it where the king couldn't interfere. Benito complied with Mirza's request, though he was most reluctant to pose as a theologian.

His host, he discovered, was powerful despite an obvious lack of manly qualities. He could swear like most men, but his tastes were all feminine: pearls instead of the masculine ruby, light colors, tea-talk in his leisure, not shop-talk. Like a woman, he kept his hands white and soft (and if possible idle), and his garments scented with perfumes of the most delicate shades.

After the usual Oriental introductions, circumlocutions, and lavish compliments, Mirza's friends began the attack. Everything Christian was assailed, that is, everything the Mohammedans had heard about. The New Testament, baptism, marriage, the Pope . . . Benito did his best to answer their objections, what any well-informed Catholic could do. He was not a theologian, he said, and he wanted it clearly understood that a defense of the Christian Law did not depend on his words.

A mullah interrupted by asking him to repeat the salutation to the Prophet after him. He then began with noisy fervor to intone the Kalimah. Benito stood there angrily, feet firmly planted, defiance in every muscle. This started a riot. A scimitar was called for and handed to the frustrated chanter of Kalimahs.

"What do you say?" he roared.

Benito turned to the one who had summoned him. "You ordered me to come to you," he said quietly, "and I am here at your command. By replying courteously to your questions, what injury have I done?"

The host looked blankly about and then he giggled stupidly. There was no harm that he could see, he said.

In the humor of the moment tempers cooled as quickly as they had flared up. The sword was exchanged for a goblet and a toast proposed. Wine flowed instead of blood.

Before he departed Mirza's palace, he had won another group of admirers, not the least of which was Mirza himself.

One would think that by this time Benito's conquest was complete. Not quite. There was a particular mullah who gloried in his reputation as a saint. The honors now paid the foreign Rume upset his pious composure and he determined to end them once and for all. Had he not by his invocations caused the deaths of a score of people? He had. And so he would curse this Abdullah. Curses, curses!

A saint's curses notwithstanding, the Abdullah's prestige increased every day. The saint could stand it no longer. Abandoning his bed of austerities, he rushed

140

about Yarkand till he found what he wanted, the Abdullah, discoursing in the midst of a crowd.

"Make way for the saint!" shouted someone on the fringe, who recognized Yarkand's holy man. "Make way for the saint!"

At last the saint confronted his foe! And best of all there were hundreds at hand to witness his triumph. All Yarkand would ring with praise before the sun had faded in its heavens.

"Give the salutation to the Prophet!" he shouted viciously, pressing a long knife against Benito's stomach. "Give the salutation or forfeit your life, you pig of a dog!"

The citizens standing about were properly horrified, but they shrugged their shoulders and said, "He is a saint. It must have been revealed to him that he would be doing God a service by killing this man. He can do no wrong—he is a saint."

A few foreign merchants among them held different views on the nature of sanctity. They disarmed the old gentleman and offered him some neat, if not polite, advice.

"I'll kill you, if it's the last thing I do!" cried the saint. He skulked through the crowd the way he had come, muttering vows and curses that would curl a man's whiskers.

It was the last Benito ever saw of him.

In Yarkand there were about a hundred mosques. On each Friday, the sacred day, all were obliged to attend prayer service five times in their respective mosques. In the early morning, heralds appeared in all the market-places, and in a loud voice they reminded the populace that it was Friday and that each had the duty of attending his mosque to say prayers according to the Koran.

141

After the heralds came the mosque-police, twelve men who carried broad leather straps attached to wooden paddles. With these they whacked all males who lacked turbans and all females who lacked their veils, and in general stirred up a rumpus which no one approved of, at least no one save the iron-handed mullahs. When the twelve policemen appeared on the streets, all who saw them in time scuttled out of sight lest even innocent things be condemned and punished. Only the Abdullah Isai held his ground. He took many a whacking and, what hurt him more, was forced to pay fines for not attending the mosque.

Tiring of this nuisance, he at last went to the king and told him that his crooked mullahs would give him no peace.

"And furthermore," he said, "I want my money back. They took my money for their fines and I want it back."

The king laughed heartily. What *would* this Abdullah do next! He promised to scold the mullahs and assured the outraged Abdullah that he was free to go everywhere he liked, and no one henceforth was to molest him.

Everywhere he liked! Benito snorted at the very idea. Everywhere he went, there were those mullahs with their long faces and longer, fuzzy beards. On all vacant squares of Yarkand they set up schools where they harangued every single day. They spread mats for the people to sit on, reserving high-chairs for themselves, and near their chairs they stuck staffs into the ground, which from time to time they grasped, raising themselves from their seats and continuing their harangues with many gesticulations. Always it was the same—unbelievers and Christians, they were wicked, their Pope was a devil, they would all go to hell. Benito got so tired of hearing himself and his brethren being consigned to hell that he felt like choking the Prophet and all his sycophants.

"Their miserable Prophet," he sputtered. "I could . . ."

VIII

At long last Hajji-Khanem, the princess-pilgrim, approached the city of Yarkand. Hearing of her coming, crowds of Yarkand's citizens flocked out to welcome her, because she was the favorite aunt of their king. In their arms they carried gifts of every kind, sweet-meats, fresh-fruits, shawls, and other items they fancied she might need, and they roared their welcome as they showered her.

Hajji-Khanem charmed them all. She graciously acknowledged their low salaams and then their gifts, too, and by the time she was done with winking and peeping at them from behind her veil, they were ready to die for her.

Like a Pied Piper she led them all in triumph to court and there she spilled out her story which had been bubbling over for months. She had suffered many misadventures. There was especially that romantic incident when a gallant Abdullah had come to her rescue when others had abandoned her. Aha! The gallant Abdullah! There was a handsome man!

And what was the Abdullah's name?

Isai!

The revelation put Yarkand's court in an uproar. Who would ever have imagined it, the quiet, determined Abdullah in the role of Prince Charming!

The Abdullah's presence was demanded in short order and the court prepared itself for a pageant of

143

approval. Yarkand would show a foreign Rume how grateful it could be, and this without a moment's delay.

When the embarrassed Benito was ushered in, the king stepped down from his throne and began the elaborate ritual of gratitude common in the East. Other courtiers joined in the hubbub, bowing and scraping, shaking their beards with eloquent flourish, while they professed on right and left that nothing could be more astonishing than this. A stranger had come to the assistance of their princess after her own countrymen had turned her down! What a marvel, indeed!

In the course of these proceedings, it was decided that a messenger should be dispatched at once to Khotan, to the princess' son. He, too, should join Yarkand's court in paying tribute to Abdullah Isai.

Khotan was eight days distant from Yarkand, so it was nearly three weeks before the prince appeared. By that time enthusiasm over the Abdullah's gallantry had long since declined, and the prince took up as if other business had called him hither. No doubt he was grateful, but he was just a boy, twenty-six years old, and the pleasures of Yarkand kept his mind fully occupied.

Hajji-Khanem reminded him of his duty and bade him invite the Abdullah for a visit. He did so and two days later Benito, armed with presents, came to call on him.

On being informed of his visitor, the prince jumped up and went out to receive him. The prince forbade Benito to bow or show other marks of obeisance, and they became fast friends at once. The prince invited his guest to be seated next to him, and then he made polite inquiries after his health and asked how old he was.

Benito said he was forty-one, a circumstance which surprised the prince because the Abdullah looked much older.

144

This was a great compliment, coming from a prince. In Asia only age included all the virtues, not wealth, and it was a great misfortune to be young. A young man was "a cub." The prince knew it well and he was much annoyed by it. He had become very self-conscious of his youth, showing it often by asking others about their age.

Since Benito was senior to him by a meager fifteen years, the prince felt a new kinship warming up inside him.

"Tell me, Abdullah Isai, where did your journey begin? Are you from Lahore?"

Benito said no, he had started from Agra.

"Why have you left your country?" the prince asked.

"To do business, Your Majesty, and to see the world." Should he mention Cathay to the prince? He decided to wait.

"What do you buy and sell?"

Benito said he had brought saffron, spices, and woolen shawls, for which reason robbers molested him less than others. He said that he hoped to obtain hemp and precious stone in Yarkand, intending thus to give a broad hint to His Majesty of Khotan.

The prince asked a great many more questions, none of them relevant to Benito's "precious stone." Benito was worried about it. He couldn't be more explicit without violating etiquette, yet he sorely needed his jade. Whether he realized it or not, he had come to identify his chances of reaching Cathay with jade. For him the jade symbolized Cathay: with it he would find Cathay; without it he would find nothing.

"Come visit me often," said the prince, terminating the audience abruptly, "and do not trouble about sending

145

word beforehand. You are always welcome. Just come before my presence and sit down without ceremony."

Benito thanked him and prepared to take his leave.

"By the way," the prince said, "I have ordered repayment in full of the amount you advanced my mother. Your jade will arrive in a few days."

Courtiers who were still in favor from one feast to another told the prince about the Abdullah's breviary. On his second visit Benito was asked to produce it, which he did with some reluctance.

"May I keep it for a few days?" the prince asked. Benito had to say yes.

The prince kept it longer than a "few days," so Benito went to ask for it.

At first the prince looked abashed. Then he said with a smile, "If I don't let you have it again, what will you do?"

"Sire," said Benito, "it is not the custom of kings to use force with their subjects."

This delighted the youngster. He rose from his pillows and motioned for Benito to follow him. As he closed the door of his private apartments, he told the guard, "No one is to come in here. We are going to discuss affairs of state."

Then he produced the breviary, kissed it, and handed it to Benito. "I beg you, read some portions aloud and explain them to me."

Benito read with great unction and tears came to the prince's eyes. Together the two talked for hours about the Pope, the manner of his election, about the way Christians make confession of their sins, of hospitals in Christian countries, of the power and majesty of kings, of bishops and cardinals, and much more.

For the prince it was a visit into another world, and

he was loath to leave it. He begged the Abdullah to return to Khotan with him.

"You have nothing to fear," he said; "my own sword shall protect you."

Benito declined, but thanked the prince for his invitation. "Perhaps some day," he said, wondering if Cathay were near the kingdom of Khotan. "Who can say where the future will carry me?"

A few days later the prince left with his mother for home. They were gone, but there was still no sign of the jade.

Besides royal audiences and salvation from the mullahs' hell, there was other business to occupy Abdullah Isai. Not for a moment had he forgotten his purpose in Yarkand and he was forever pestering people with questions. Have you heard of Cathay? Cambaluc? Where were the lost Christians of Friar John?

In Yarkand he found evidence enough that his trail was getting warm. In the markets he bought paper fans, sticks of ink, porcelain, and rhubarb, all guaranteed "Cathayan" by the respective proprietors. In another bazaar he discovered paintings on paper which represented a man wearing a biretta (a hat like Xavier's) with cross attached. Before this appropriately Christian garb another "Christian" stood at attention with folded hands, and the two of them swooned in ecstasy.

"A bishop," Benito finally decided.

On a porcelain dish he found a "Franciscan" monk hanging by his girdle, with what might have been a tonsure on his head, though (how is this?) he wore the long beard of a Chinaman. That a Christian Franciscan was dead, hung by his own girdle, did not appear to be significant. The tonsure was the important thing, and so was the girdle.

Like any good detective, Benito carefully checked Yarkand's jails. Most Oriental jails were reserved for foreigners and he hoped that among these "guests" he would find at least one honest-to-goodness Cathayan.

In one cell he found a captive king, one time ruler of Tibet, now star-prisoner (these three years) of the benevolent Yarkand administration. He languished under his hard lot and his harder name, "Compo Namgyal," and he wrestled valiantly with all who came to him; for he couldn't speak Persian, but only Tibetan. Benito visited him often, determined to batter down the language barrier. All that he accomplished could be summed up in one word: "Angil," something vaguely familiar, but not clearly an idea.

But another Tibetan turned up in the same jail. His name was Lunrique and, being a physician, he knew medicine and Persian to boot.

This Lunrique told Benito that in his homeland there was no rite of circumcision like the Mohammedan's, but that on the eighth day children were taken to the temple, and that their Itolama washed them and named them after the saints which were painted in their churches. He also said that their chief Father, whom they called "Kon-chog," wore a mitre on his head and a robe which resembled a chasuble. The people observed a fast of forty days during which they abstained from food till nightfall and took neither wine nor meat. They had the "Angil," which means Evangelia, or Gospel. Their priests never married and all believed in Judgment Day and in eight hells and three paradises, each of which had an impossible-to-remember name. In conclusion, the physician assured de Goes that some Tibetan grandees then resided in Cathay, which was only a month's

148

journey from Tibet, and that those in Cathay would be very glad to see Abdullah Isai.

"Get me out of here," he quipped, "and I will show you the way myself!"

During that spring, the struggle for a caravan formation dragged on interminably. It was like organizing a new government, with seventy-seven politicians jockeying for as many lucrative positions. A premier, a cabinet, and a seventy-two man congress. In this case, however, the organizing took the pattern of each one's ability to pay.

The right of leading a caravan to China was sold by the king of Kashgar to the highest bidder, whom he appointed as his ambassador. Then, for a consideration, the leader associated himself with four others who retained the same title. Finally he enrolled a group of seventy-two merchants who bribed him generously to be included in this number. Those who paid but little were excluded. To all who brought him presents, the crafty ambassador pledged his word—which afterwards he often broke. Only seventy-two, alas, could enter China with him.

Thus the caravan took on the appearances of a diplomatic mission, for only in this guise could it penetrate that proud, mysterious land of China.

The "diplomatic mission's" tribute to the emperor of China was determined by custom. There were to be one thousand arobas of jade, three hundred and forty horses, three hundred small diamonds, one hundred pounds of fine blue pigment, six hundred knives, six hundred files, all of which totaled in value approximately seven thousand crowns. In return, the Son of Heaven made acknowledgment to the tune of fifty thousand crowns. A six-fold profit.

149

So for many months merchants dickered and bargained. Who would contribute the diamonds? The knives? The jade?

There was Benito, right back at his problem. His jade. There was only one way of getting that jade—go after it. That's exactly what Benito determined to do.

I X

Camels, poor things, have no childhood. They are born in sophistication and gravity and in these spirits they continue till their sad demise. Unlike colts or calves, baby camels eschew any such levity as romping. They simply lie about or stand in the way for eight long years before gaining strength to carry life's burdens.

The Asiatic says that a camel comes by his gravity and superior airs quite honestly. There are a hundred names for God, he explains. Man knows only ninety-nine and the camel knows the hundredth. So he holds his head high and now and then condescends to acknowledge humans with a supercilious nod.

Whatever the reason, Benito could never accept the camel's lack of humility. There was a donkey and a cow at Christ's manger, he recalled, both humble beasts; but no camel. At least not till the Magi arrived. The camel was a worldly animal, proud as well as stupid.

Benito had long since come to be resigned to the camel's clumsiness, his slow lumbering ways, his odors, repelling and omnipresent like the smell of bilge inside a ship. To his fine airs, never. And because of this, he tried to get along without him.

But a camel could not always be dispensed with. Benito had to face it. In late spring, 1604, he went out and bought six two-humped males, one as white as a cloud and others in varying shades of brown. All were rested and fat and eager for a journey abroad.

Since Isaac was to stay in Yarkand to guard the Abdullah's possessions, camel-boys had to be hired also, and Benito obtained two. Both were Mohammedans, but similarities ended there. One was an old fellow, bent and wrinkled beyond his years. Like Benito he had had much to suffer, but the process didn't mellow him. Patience, a kind of sugar, had been wanting and the disposition of old Talbas had become disagreeable, even bitter to take.

But Yogda made up for him. He was just a lovable boy, fifteen years old, born and raised in Persia. He had left home "to see the world," a fact which endeared him to Benito all the more.

Yogda was very poor. He bound and laced his feet in sheepskin; his cotton pants had been bright once, but faded now; his shirt, loose and patched, did poor service; and even his headcloth, drawn back from the temples by a braid of camel's hair, was a hand-me-down. Poor as it was, Yogda took great pride in it. It was a *man's* head-cloth, wasn't it?

But Yogda was rich in other things: personality, imagination, hopes. He had ideas. He knew a lot about the countryside, especially local legends, which cast a spell over him like a witch's abracadabra. He believed them all as readily as he believed the mullahs. Almost nothing was too fantastic to be accepted. In Yogda's world there was always a place for black magic and monsters with human vices.

In early June, Benito got started. Boys by the dozen were on hand, their usual Oriental passivity shaken by the tinkling-bell of a caravan. When the lead-camel

151

passed the last bazaar, a money-changer threw a copper over its head and shouted, "Happy journey." Yogda was pleased, for he said that it was a good omen. They would return without mishap.

It took several hours of steady plodding to clear the environs of Yarkand. By this time the sun was high. On all sides lay the scorching desert, the southern rim of the terrible Takla-Makan. Sand-dunes stretched endlessly, like great swells on the sea, sometimes sixty or ninety feet high. The silence was interrupted only by the soughing of the wind and heavy breathing of the beasts.

The camels had started to molt and they looked like ancient and stuffed animals that were falling apart. Great patches of camel-hair, this was the stuff of commerce, had been shed already, leaving the poor beasts quite naked. They took this, a robbery of nature, in the best spirit possible. They were too stupid to protest. They plopped their wide-spreading soft feet up and down in effortless rhythm, snatched at scraggly tamarisk as they passed, chewing them raw, and were seemingly oblivious to all the inconveniences of a desert trek.

Yogda kept up his chatter. On the left, he said, there had once been a mighty city. An ancient king of these lands, shocked by the eccentricities of a holy old man, had caused him to be buried in sand up to his mouth. Judgment fell upon the kingdom, because winds blew and sands came from the heavens, burying forever the fertile plains that had been there.

"May Allah be praised!" said Yogda in conclusion.

He had other stories, lots of them. Most had a moral, but Yogda seemed to be unconcerned with this aspect. He told just to be telling.

Had the Abdullah ever heard of the city called Takla-Makan, Yogda asked very earnestly.

No, the Abdullah hadn't.

"Well," said Yogda, "once in the midst of this desert," his hand swept the bleak yellow sea to the east, "there was an ancient city buried in the sands. Among the ruins of its mosques and palaces and houses there were great ingots of gold and lumps of silver. And it was all out in the open and anybody could see it. But if a caravan went there and loaded its camels with gold, the drivers would be enchanted. Instead of going in a straight line, they would walk round and round in a circle till they died. The only way the enchantment could be broken was to throw the gold away."

He looked slyly at the Abdullah. "Do you believe that story?" he asked.

"Well now, I don't know," said Benito; "one hears a good many stories."

"I believe it," said Yogda fervently. "May Allah protect me." He waited a bit and started again.

"It is said," he began, "that once a lone man went to that city and loaded his camel with gold. When he started to leave, a thousand wild-cats came right out of the thin air and scratched and bit him. So he threw away the gold and the cats vanished forever."

The Takla-Makan, all Yogda's hearers had to agree, was now as fertile for producing ghosts and evil spirits as it once had been for producing barley.

When evening came, Talbas and Yogda pitched a couple of tents, spread mats and blankets for beds, and cooked a frugal meal. Yogda told more stories. They were like seasoning, always sprinkled in the right measure and always salty, bringing with them peace and repose in every digestive organ.

"Just the thing," thought Benito dreamily before

153

falling asleep. "Just the thing to go with rice and mutton after a hot, sweaty day."

On the fourth day a strong eastern wind rose over the desert. Soon it was a gale, and a yellow haze floated above the horizon. Colors faded and distances became distorted. Sand dunes appeared to be distant mountains brooding behind veils of flying sand. Day had turned into night. There was nothing to do but make camp till the morrow.

Storms like this were common enough on the Takla-Makan. No one was alarmed, even if all were annoyed, camels included. The greatest problem was to keep the camels from catching cold, a misfortune to which they easily succumbed when molting. To lose one, even by cold, was bad luck, said Yogda; at any price the camels had to keep warm.

"And how about us?" asked Benito, not greatly impressed by Yogda's threats of consequences.

That night Benito used his own blankets.

By morning the wind had subsided and Yogda's chatter, as well as the journey, took up where it had left off.

"Soon we will see the fields and gardens of Khotan. Rice, the best in all Asia," he said enthusiastically. "And apricots!" His eyes rolled heavenward and his arms went up with them. "They will be ripe when we get there. Grapes—these people make wine, you know—do you approve of wine?"

"Yes," said Benito, "if it's good. Is this wine good?"

"To be honest, no." Yogda made a wry face. "It tastes like vinegar. You shall see. Khotan has pears and apples and cotton—many other things. It has been said," Yogda used that caution-phrase frequently, "that Khotan Province is more fertile than Kashmir, though

154

I do not know for myself. I have never been to Kashmir. Some day, perhaps. . . ."

An after-thought. "Have you been to Kashmir?"

"Yes, I've been to Kashmir," Benito nodded, and Yogda drew his breath in. Here was a man to admire—he had *been* places!

X

Khotan was off the beaten paths and that meant only one thing, intolerance. Especially intolerance in religion. It was the city's boast that no "Giaours" penetrated its sanctuary and lived to tell of it. As a matter of plain fact, the boast was an honest one. Except for de Goes, no Westerner from Marco Polo till the nineteenth century did visit Khotan and live to tell of it. There had been some who tried, during that long interval, but they never came back.

Benito's immunity came partly from the king's promised protection. Mostly it derived from his courage. Even the fervent Mohammedans, who, according to their neighbors, were eager to drink the blood of Christians, could not bring themselves to kill his courage, with or without royal approval.

Benito took Khotan the way he took Yarkand. Though he had his lodgings near the caravansary (the better to keep his eye on the inscrutable Talbas), he made the town his own. He dined with the king, and with equal poise defied the mullahs or showered street urchins with candies and coppers. No one could be indifferent to him—they either hated or admired.

And just when the battle about his person had reached

155

a climax, without the least concern he took off to visit Khotan's "secret," its jade quarries.

Jade in the Orient had but one source: remote Khotan. Marco Polo had "discovered" this source; that is to say, he visited the place during his wanderings. "There are rivers in this country," he wrote, "in which quantities of jasper and chalcedony are found." That's all—supreme nonchalance before one of the wonders of his contemporary world.

Marco's jasper and chalcedony were jade: the former, "jaspis" of the ancient Greeks, and the latter, a green jade with its own name.

Even in Marco's time, jade was highly prized by the Chinese. Their craftsmen, with exquisite taste, cut it into trinkets and ornaments, vases, bracelets, buckles, snuff-boxes, and so on. They called it yu-stone and ascribed to it special powers. Men and women kept bracelets as amulets against sickness, a mild superstition which passed on even to Europe, where it assumed other forms. Europeans, for example, enclosed bits of jade in the foundations of buildings as a security against lightning.

There were two kinds of jade to be had in different places. Benito visited the Khotan River first, not far from the city. He found the river divided up into claims, like mining claims, and divers were active in each of the sections. They were naked and they dived into the icy waters (off the "Roof of the World") in the same manner that divers fish for pearls. They brought up jade in the shape of large pebbles, worn and water-rolled by countless centuries.

The other less valuable kind was hewn out of near-by mountains. It cost an incredible amount of labor to cut the stone in large slabs, six feet broad, because of its hardness and the remoteness of the spot. Benito noted that they built fires on the cut-area before operations, this to reduce the hardness at least a trifle.

Some of the jade was white as milk, some dark green like the most beautiful emeralds, others yellow, vermilion, and jet-black. The most highly prized pieces were the white speckled with red and green veined with gold.

All this Benito recorded in his journal. He added drily that if he had to carry jade all the way to China, it had better be green and gold.

Back in Yarkand, a month had passed since de Goes' departure. There was no definite word regarding his welfare. Only rumors, ugly rumors as tenuous as wisps of smoke, floated back to Isaac who awaited him. Abdullah Isai, these reports would have it, was dead. He had been called upon to address Allah's Prophet, and refusing, had been torn to pieces by Allah's priests.

Poor Isaac's grief was boundless. For whole days he did nothing but weep. Benito murdered! His body, bloody and torn by beasts, a heap of flesh in the dust! Was life without the Brother worth living?

Out across the city, within gray walls of the Buddhist monastery, there was great rejoicing, because, according to law, the property of deceased travellers fell to the monks. The Abdullah, a rich man, was already a week overdue, they gloated. Surely the monastery would soon fall heir to his wealth. And the monks beat the drum.

Some of the more sanguine paid Isaac numerous and unwelcome visits. They had come, they explained, to examine the Abdullah's possessions. Did the servant Isaac know the law?

The law! Isaac knew it well.

Where were the Abdullah's treasures, his bales of priceless things, and the little book? Was this all? Why

157

the Abdullah was a rich man, everyone knew that! Was the servant Isaac concealing his master's effects?

But the law gave the Abdullah more time, a little more time.

Oh yes, quite true. The monks would return. Their respects to the servant Isaac.

Then one evening, Benito came riding on his camel. He had bags full of jade, choicest cuts as gifts from his princess-pilgrim. Special credentials and passports urged by the grateful prince-son. Isaac in his ecstatic joy frisked everywhere. Now let those monks come snooping around! Hah!

All the triumph of Asia was in his laugh.

XI

Agi-Afis was like a juggernaut: he moved slowly, but his progress was certain. He was always sure of himself. That's why he was one of the richest men in the capital and could easily afford to bribe when bribing was expedient.

There was, for example, his determination to be ambassador to China. Merchants (and Agi-Afis was a merchant) looked to China as the culmination of their commerce. They achieved this climax by investing wisely, by risking their fortune on the King of Kashgar's appointment, and finally by risking their necks along the trail of a pseudo-diplomatic mission to China.

Agi-Afis understood all this very well. In a glowing anticipation of a seven-fold return, he posted a "gift" that would assure his appointment, two hundred bags of musk, and began to hatch his plans for the journey.

Of course he was right; Agi-Afis never reckoned in

error. The credentials were his. Next he needed suitable companionship, not just the money-conscious, selfish confrere of the market. He wanted ingenuity and courage, and he knew where to find it. His man was Abdullah Isai. All that was lacking was the Abdullah's consent, and the Juggernaut felt sure of it.

Benito had been careful to keep secret his intention of proceeding to China. He knew his services were eagerly sought, but for one thing, he couldn't compete in bribe-bidding with the wealthy locals who clamored for inclusion in the caravan. Could he get a berth without an exorbitant bribe? He would stall and see.

He had not long to wait. Agi-Afis soon appeared on his threshold, the suave, impassive Oriental, begging for admission to Benito's quarters.

Would the Abdullah Isai consider a journey to Peking?

The Abdullah Isai was not sure. You see, he had applied to the king for a safe-conduct to the kingdom of Cialis, just east of Kashgar. Besides, if he did go to China, some of his companions of the Kabul caravan had been urging him to remain with them. They were making plans to go to that illustrious land of the East— they would surely have a prosperous journey. No, the Abdullah Isai was not sure. But his undying gratitude (bows and appropriate smiles) to the most excellent Abdullah Agi-Afis.

Did the Abdullah Isai know of the emperor's conditions for the journey to China? The Son of Heaven paid ambassadors' expenses of the road, besides handsome gifts. These gifts were worth a fortune.

Benito's eyes widened a little. Was the Abdullah Agi-Afis offering him a position as one of five ambassadors?

159

Indeed, and the Abdullah Isai would do well to accept so handsome an offer. Now let him but gift the caravan leader—jade? Some musk, perhaps?

Benito refused to commit himself. He gave Agi-Afis little encouragement, and the offended Juggernaut rolled away and on to the king's palace. He demanded a royal order that Abdullah Isai accompany his mission to China. The king sent for Benito.

"Abdullah Isai," the king began, "you've received an honorable offer to accompany my mission to the court at Peking. Do you not wish to go to Peking?"

"Sire," replied Benito, "my old friends of the Kabul caravan wish to retain me. Besides, this Peking journey is long and tedious."

"Would the Abdullah be willing if I gave special orders to free you from old obligations?"

"Sire, the Abdullah is your obedient servant; I will go willingly if you do this and," he paused for emphasis, "provide me with a safe-conduct for the entire journey."

In the end, Agi-Afis secured Benito's services, but it was perfectly evident to all that Benito, not the ambassador, was the one granting a favor.

At this point Demetrius showed up, the tall deacon who had left Benito's party at Kabul. He had come to Yarkand after all, and now he was greeting Benito and Isaac with all the warmth of his Grecian heart. He would go to Cathay, too, he said, if only Benito would accept him as a member of the caravan.

Benito and Isaac were delighted with Demetrius' arrival. He was a good fellow, even if a bit chicken-hearted, and, more to his credit, he was a Christian and deacon besides. They were glad to have him. But joy over the reunion was short-lived; Demetrius was soon to be in trouble.

160

According to custom, the newly-formed caravan held a kind of carnival, during which festivities one of the merchants was elected "emperor." All the others paid him homage, offering presents and bowing to him with good grace and willing laughter. But Demetrius, to save his pocket, held back. The "emperor" promptly slapped him into prison and threatened a good flogging. It was Benito who finally got him off. With tact and some presents out of his own supply he talked the "emperor" into releasing Demetrius and giving him a full pardon.

The deacon now roamed about Yarkand, protected somewhat by the Abdullah Isai's patronage, and he questioned everybody about the advisability of proceeding with the caravan. He just couldn't make up his mind, at least not without asking everyone.

People of Yarkand spoke up to this friend of the Abdullah. They said they did not like to see the Abdullah killed, but he surely would be killed if he tried to go beyond Yarkand. They said that they admired the Abdullah's courage and daring. They would like to see the Abdullah succeed, but he didn't have a chance. The Abdullah would be killed. His servant Isaac would be killed. And Demetrius, if he accompanied them, would be killed too. That's what the people of Yarkand had to say, and they hoped that Demetrius would persuade the Abdullah to turn back.

Demetrius was shaken in his very roots. In a panic of fear he sought out Benito and told him that he had changed his mind. He did not wish to go beyond Yarkand for this and that and those reasons, and especially, he added, because he did not want to be killed.

Benito said all right, it would not change matters much.

161

"Oh, my Brother," the distracted deacon cried. "Do not go farther! They will kill you—people have told me this. Come back to India with me. Come back!"

Benito said no, he would not let himself be deterred by fear of death from the duty of obedience, much less would he do so now in a business from which so much glory to God might be expected. He said it would be most unworthy conduct to frustrate the hopes of so many for fear of death and to throw away all the expense that had been incurred by others. He hoped still to carry through the project with the help of Him who had thus far brought him prosperously, but in any case he would rather risk his neck in the cause than draw back from his purpose.

Again and again Demetrius tried to persuade Benito. Come back, come back before it is too late! Benito held fast and Demetrius finally withdrew, ashamed of himself, but unable to summon the courage to go to Cathay.

Once again there was only Isaac.

Departure preparations were begun. Benito and Isaac, after a whole year's delay in Yarkand, were chafing to be on their way again, and they packed and checked their provisions and bales with the light-heartedness of boys leaving school. Yogda was still with them—he was going as far as Aksu—and the happy little fellow worked like a Trojan to prove that he was indispensable.

On the twelfth of November, Agi-Afis ordered a final inspection. They would leave on the morrow, he said.

But on the morrow, before they got started, a courier arrived with the news that a Yarkand-bound caravan from China was nearing the city. Would the royal embassy await? It would. Agi-Afis called a day's delay, and the camel-boys all rushed back to their sweethearts, grateful for anything that fortune brought them.

When the incoming caravan finally straggled into Yarkand's north-side caravansary, Benito, as well as Agi-Afis, hurriedly sought out its leaders. "Any news of Cathay?" he asked them.

No, the new arrivals told him, they didn't know about Cathay. They had been to a place where people were "Cafares," that is, people without a law. Some there were in that place called "Franks." They were foreigners from the east and much despised. But Cathay, no, they had heard nothing of Cathay nor of priests who wore strange hats on their heads. Sorry.

The next day, on the fourteenth of November, 1604, Benito plunged deeper into the deserts of Asia.

A caravan starting from Yarkand makes choice between two routes, both skirting the edge of the Tarim Basin of eastern Turkestan. This vast basin is but a link of desert-chain that spans the Old World, from the western Sahara, eastward, to eastern Asia within the confines of China. All around the Tarim Basin rise fantastic mountain ranges, like walls of a prison, leaving open only one door, a break through the east, where the great sea of sand pours itself into another, into the Gobi.

Whether one skirted the north rim or the east, as Marco Polo had done, there were dangers and treacheries common to both, and troubles so annoying that the traveller was always tempted to wish he had taken the other way. Both routes offered certain advantages, but because the north was more direct to Peking, most caravans followed it, leaving the east to those who travelled just to see the world, like Marco Polo.

The north road weaved in and out of the foothills along the Tian Shan Mountains, thence to the very limits of the range and across the Gobi at a relatively narrow

163

point. Because of the mountains, water could usually be found by digging a few feet under the sands, and the poplar forests in the foothills provided protection from robbers, as well as some game. Wild boars were there in abundance. Deer, too, red deer and roe deer, which hunters pursued for their antlers, much cherished as a kind of medicine. Besides these there were foxes, wolves, lynxes, hares, and lots of tigers.

It was the north route that Agi-Afis determined to follow. He was much given to the pleasures offered in city or village life—along the Tian Shan Mountains there would not be many nights in the open. Villages were strung out interminably, like priests in long procession, each one upholding a religious tradition, as with candle flaming he marched along the path of time. The religious tradition was Agi-Afis', or enough like it that he could feel at home wherever he pitched for the night, unless it be under the open skies. In the latter case, it was Benito who could feel more at home, Benito and the simple shepherd guides who almost made a religion of the wide open spaces. They were dreamers and stargazers with the smell of sheep dung in their rough, sheepskin trousers, much too rustic for the fastidious Agi-Afis. Well might he prefer his urban life, and the north route.

So along the Tian Shan the caravan started its crawl. Camels, Bactrian and two-humped, like the camels Benito drove to Khotan, were tied in strings of eight; and wherever the desert was wide enough, they were led in parallel columns more than thirty camels wide. They were in fine fettle, well covered with hair that hung shaggy like Spanish moss, especially below their chins. A stranger quite instinctively wanted to jerk these beards and say, "There old boy, take that!" but he

164

never dared. The camel-boys would have protested. They loved their animals with touching tenderness and wept bitterly when one would die.

The weather was tolerable—clear, cool days with frosty nights. Swamps or marshes along the way were always frozen over in the morning, a circumstance which bothered no one very much. Sometimes winds came up during the day and fine sand blew about like an ocean spray. But there were no great storms during this stretch. Only a bleakness, a soul-trying monotony of sand, tamarisk, which the camels chewed raw, and scattered boulders.

The caravan met shepherds, timid silent creatures characterized mostly by an overwhelming fear of tigers.

Benito and Isaac often talked with them. One day, after a chat with a shepherd, Isaac rejoined Benito, rollicking with laughter.

"What happened?" said Benito.

"I asked him how far the desert went," said Isaac. He laughed some more.

"And?" said Benito, impatient for the funny part.

"The shepherd said, 'In that direction to the end of the world—and it takes three months to get there.'"

Twenty-five days after leaving Yarkand, Agi-Afis' caravan arrived at Aksu in a cloud of dust. Aksu was propitious to Benito. Its king was a twelve-year-old, a boy very much like Yogda, and a cousin of Kashgar's king. Benito took care to pay a prompt visit to this young cousin of his Yarkand benefactor. Lacking suitable gifts for boys, he brought as the next best thing bags of candy.

"Whee!" cried the royal Tom Thumb. He was soon captivated by this merchant who knew so well just what boys liked to talk about. After sampling his candy,

165

he clapped for dancers—melody, rhythm for the new found friend, the Abdullah!

Benito watched a score of Turki maidens brightly clad in reds, purples, greens. To please the court, he kept time with the music and bowed gallantly to the whirling performers.

"Now you dance," said the boy.

Benito danced a fast, gay tango learned in his faraway home. At forty-three, hard work this dancing! He soon tired and came huffing and puffing to the king.

"You must come tomorrow," the entranced little fellow commanded.

For fifteen days Benito often made visits to the boy-king, to his tutor and guardian who helped the boy rule, to the boy's mother, to whom Benito gave a number of mirrors!

They were all entranced and insisted that the Abdullah remain with them, but Benito could not. Caravans, like tides and suns, wait for no man. On Christmas Eve he again took to the deserts which for a thousand miles stretched across Asia before him.

XII

At times Benito was as much alone as Robinson Crusoe on a lost island. He found himself in a strange new world, new even to him, with no remnants save his memories to cushion him in moments of shock. Now, just what was there to soften life's hazards? Could it be novelty? Perhaps, but even the taste for novelty was satiated in years of travel.

In the last analysis, Benito had only his religion to rely

166

on, to steady himself when his sands were shifting too fast for adjustment.

Especially these last days, Isaac noted great changes in the Jesuit. His strong physique had broken down and he was often sick with the "fever." No longer did dangers of the trail even occur to him. There were other trials far more formidable, overpowering, destructive—a persecution, for example, by those on whom he relied most for support, his caravan companions. They were "Moors," he often told himself; what else could be expected? Yet, subconsciously, Benito expected something vastly different. He expected fellowship and a share in hardships as well as joy. It was unthinkable that his own fellow-travellers would try to rob him, but that was a fact. There were thieves within his own household. He possessed a king's ransom in jade, and his treasure made all the world his enemy, all but Isaac, who was half his soul.

The world was hostile. It envied and coveted—and only time stood between the jade and its changing proprietorship. Another master, another man against the world by reason of the pearl-of-great-price. Did no one realize the burden of riches? No one save the rich, who were too weak to unburden themselves.

Benito would gladly have yielded his treasure. It was, alas, his only assurance of arriving at Cathay, his only ticket through gates and past hungry vultures who guarded them. If others would covet and threaten, then he must stand guard himself. To yield now would be weakness, and weakness was certain death.

So Benito found himself very much alone in that new world—not just the world of scrawny tamarisk bushes, or poplar forests hiding queer sheep-skin-covered shepherds, or yellow sand-dunes in ceaseless waves to the east, or even in the stifling dusts and dryness of the Tarim Basin. All these were foreign enough to one suckled by the seashore. But outlook, the climate of human habit and expression—this isolated him from men. This placed him on a little island and cut him off from communication and understanding and sympathy when it was needed most.

As Benito's spirits sagged the more, his caravan progressed from village to village with certain, if slow, steps toward the northeast and Cathay. The farther from Yarkand he moved, the more wretched the villages became till there were only struggling hamlets, desperately clinging to the trail, thirsty for the elixir of trade. Without it they'd have perished, like the forests of poplar scattered along the fringe of the Takla-Makan.

Everywhere Benito inquired for news of the lost empire and everywhere he was told the same tale, over and over.

Yes, in the middle of the desert there had been an ancient city; it had many people, was powerful, and its riches were scarcely to be believed. But sandstorms came up. They blew for weeks and the city with its great numbers was buried forever.

Ruins? Yes, there were ruins still to be seen, poking up here and there in the sands. Tips of towers and walls, and among them (so everyone said), gold and long bars of silver. . . .

A lost city? Cambaluc? Perhaps this was Cambaluc which had been buried in the desert. Who could say? The Abdullah, if he valued his life, dared not go near, because he would be bewitched and never return again to his home.

By mid-February of 1605, the caravan had reached the more imposing oasis of Kuchar. Here Agi-Afis called another halt of one month to give men and animals a badly needed rest. The heavy loads and want of food had exhausted the strength of all.

In some respects Kuchar was considered the most pleasant town in all the Tarim Basin. Groves of poplars and shady lanes lent a peaceful, bucolic air to the place, but its peace escaped Benito from the start. Mohammedan priests harangued and vexed him almost every moment. Their fanaticism knew no limits. They made efforts to prolong arguments day and night, and though Benito managed to sink his share of theology's subtle shafts, the subsequent unpleasantness made it scarcely worth the effort. When they departed in March, Benito was glad to see the last of Kuchar's poplars sketched against a grey sky.

When, twenty-five days later, he reached another important oasis, he discovered that he had not left all Mohammedan priests behind. Here again he was among worthy brothers of their Kuchar confreres.

The place was called "Cialis" by de Goes, probably the modern Karashar, on a river which flowed from a large near-by lake. It was a small town, but strategically important because it held a mountain pass on the only road between Aksu and the Gobi. A Mohammedan garrison kept quarters there, a fact which intimidated mostly the purses of travellers.

The king of Cialis was another relative of Kashgar's monarch. Unlike cousin Tom Thumb's, his first encounter with Abdullah Isai threatened to be most unfavorable, but the latter carefully plotted his gifting and bribe-strategy, which, as always, achieved the desired effect.

The Abdullah, weary and half-sick, was determined to get in Cialis what he had not taken from Kuchar: a

169

rest. Camels got rest. Donkeys and horses got rest. Camel-boys, merchants, everybody got rest, but the weary, weary Abdullah Isai. For him repose was that elusive nectar which escaped him most when he sought its sweetness most diligently. But he would find it in Cialis—to this end he would avoid all manner of argument.

One night when the king and several of his priests were discussing religion, some one got the idea that Abdullah Isai should be called in. He was sent for. Issac received the messenger as an omen of evil and tried to dissuade Benito from going.

"Uh huh," mumbled the Abdullah sleepily, and he followed the nocturnal visitor to court.

As soon as he walked in, the priests opened a fierce attack. They blasted away at everything Christian, and Benito the warrior battled away like any indignant Catholic. After a stormy session the king suddenly clapped his hands and called for silence.

"Enough!" he cried. "Leave this man in peace. After all, he too is a believer as all Christians are. For they," he nodded toward the Abdullah, "are followers of a religion which at one time was professed by our forefathers."

It was true. The king made reference to Nestorianism which had penetrated China in the seventh century. Nestorian Christian communities had been common in some parts of that ancient world. Now there were traces of it, very few traces, for like the sands which buried desert cities Mohammedanism blew in along the trails and buried perhaps forever the religion of their forefathers.

The reference startled Benito as well, and he questioned the king carefully. Was this, then, Cathay of Master Polo's day? It was not—it took no time at all to

170

uncover that fact. The ancients of the oasis, on whom the court relied for its traditions, could narrate accounts of Nestorianism a thousand years old. They could tell of Buddhism, its struggle, its collapse, of the religion of the Prophet which came along with the bales of merchants. Of Marco Polo's Christianity there was not the slightest vestige.

Agi-Afis, Benito one day discovered, was deliberately holding up the caravan in Cialis for his own ends. Some of his associates in the embassy had dropped out, and the Juggernaut refused to roll again till he had replaced them with other wealthy and generous pretenders. In a word, Agi-Afis was demanding more money.

Benito, his patience worn thin by priestly annoyances, pleaded with the king for permission to start without the others. Of course, Agi-Afis opposed this prospect with all the eloquence of his purse, since with the Abdullah would go a neat half-ton of jade.

But the king favored Benito, and he presented him with all needed permissions and passports.

Benito quickly hired more camel-drivers and a few servants. With Isaac he set forth in the lightest mood he had known for many moons. At last he was master of his own caravan. He could choose or dismiss as occasion required, and best of all he could say his Christian prayers in peace.

Two days later he began to regret his new freedom. About four in the afternoon of that day, a Saturday, the solemn monotony of the desert was broken by distant vague sounds and a cloud of dust on the horizon. Benito was alarmed and called a halt to discuss the matter with his guides. While they talked, a string of horses silhouetted like a frieze against the sky came into view on a distant ridge. Bandits maybe?

171

One guide suggested that they silence their own caravan bells by taking them off the camels. Then by listening carefully they could tell whether the others were friend or foe. Bells were like flags on ships. They revealed all that was needed.

Some one else said there was no time to do this. If they were robbers, the horsemen could be upon their victims in a few minutes. On the other hand, he said, if they were friendly, they would soon reveal that too, because they would camp on the meadow below, in full view, not hiding nor waiting for others to appear.

Benito ordered his party to conceal themselves behind sand-dunes. They should hide and watch the strangers' movements till some indication of purpose was given.

Meanwhile the advancing horsemen had observed the approach and tactics of Benito's caravan.

"Surely," the leader, a long-whiskered old fellow, told his companions, "these are robbers come to kill us. We'll stay behind sand-dunes till we learn of their intentions."

He ordered all to stay close together; and when the time came to fight with great courage, "Fight for your very lives!" he urged them with suitable gestures.

The two opposing parties continued to duck in and out of dunes to reconnoitre, and this went on till the scouts of one party discovered the purpose of the other. A parley was called and the good news was out. Friends! Laughing joyfully and with gestures of mock battle the two caravans fell upon one another. It was a huge joke! Who would believe that they had wasted an hour hiding from each other! Then questions came like a torrent, but nobody stopped to answer. Old Whiskers suggested that everybody camp together in the meadow so that gossip of the trail could flow till the morrow.

The meadow was spacious and there was plenty of

172

water for animals of both caravans. Tents were hastily pitched. Argols were gathered and lit, a meal was soon steaming in pots, and men were hovering over them, famished after the day's excitement.

As the sun dropped beyond the western dune-ridge, these men from the East gobbled rice and boiled mutton and melons and chattered gaily with men from the West. They drank their heavy oversweet tea and poked the argols, burning brightly now with a bluish red flame. The night got colder as it got darker. Fires were unconsciously hugged, but all was forgotten in the warmth of conversation.

For the whole night the babble went on. No one thought of sleep. When trail gossip gave out, the campers took to boasting. They told tales of the desert as weird as any of those swapped by old sea salts under yardarms and mizzenmast. There were stories of murders and smuggling and hunting and the hero of each was always the one who told it. One told about the time he had been chased by seven wolves. With Allah's aid, he said, he had killed one and the rest pounced upon it and devoured it while he got away. Another had hunted lions, travelling through the jungles on an elephant. He had found and killed two cubs when the lioness appeared, foaming with fury. She climbed right up where he stood on the elephant and but for Allah's aid he would have been killed on the spot. Allah gave him strength to beat off that lioness with a club. Praise to Allah.

The day's misadventure provoked robber talk. On that subject a great deal had to be said. There were robbers who had cannons; there were robbers who slit men open and took their hearts out, even before they were dead. All robbers carried huge curved swords with which they could cut a man's head off as if it were made

173

of wax. Some robbers drank human blood and others dressed like generals in the army, like the emperor himself, someone was willing to swear.

"I have heard how robbers are recruited for their dirty work," said a camel-driver shyly, in a low voice.

"Hear him, hear him!" cried his neighbor, to quell the babble and give the shy one a chance. The neighbor was an energetic little man with a voice like a bugle. One blast from that assertive instrument commanded instant attention; so silence fell over the crowd, while the shy one self-consciously cleared his throat.

"I have heard how robbers are recruited," he said. It was a story often repeated with local variations, but all wanted to hear it again.

"When the robbers see a lusty youth," the shy one began, "they tempt him with the hope of riches, bringing him to such a point that he would kill his father with his own hand. They get him drunk on wine, then they carry him to a robbers' den where he is charmed with delicious music and beautiful women, and they leave him here several days. But when he falls asleep, they carry him back to his old surroundings. After he awakes, they ask him what he has seen, and he tells them. Then they say that is Paradise and that it is just as the Prophet described it in his law. Then with prayers and texts they induce that youth to join them so that he may regain Paradise.

"And that's the way they get robber recruits," said the shy one.

At this point a little dog trotted up, shivering and whining because it was cold. Suddenly they all realized that the fire had gone down and that they were cold too.

During these festivities Brother de Goes had followed his own course. The evening for him was the climax in

174

a drama. The mists of Cathay would be dissipated during the night. By dawn Cathay would cease to exist forever and credit for its destruction would redound to a chance paper, a souvenir of Portuguese writing snatched up in Ricci's Peking garden. All that followed would be anti-climax, the swift downward motion of drama's finis, and by the same stroke, Benito's finis. It was his act. He would pass away with its last curtain.

Benito hadn't expected the eventuality. So often he had asked the same questions, received the same vague, improbable replies! He had almost ceased hoping. What could these caravaneers from Peking say that others he had met could not say? Ah well, if a needle be lost for straw, will not constant plucking reveal it?

Before supper was served, Benito had been about his business. He had warmed up to it in approved Oriental fashion. The trail, the weather, the Abdullah from Peking. The Abdullah from Peking, an Armenian, bronzed by countless suns, graciously drank to Benito's health while he fondly stroked his beard. That beard was like a flag, and Benito chuckled softly as he examined the friendly face behind it.

At length he popped the question, calmly, not really expecting the answer he received. Had the most excellent Abdullah been to Cathay?

"Cathay?" Old Whiskers asked. "To be sure we have been to Cathay." He looked to the east. "Almost to the shores of the sea in that direction—Peking, and the land called China."

"Is this, then, Cathay?" de Goes said.

"It is," very gravely. "I have been there and I have lived in the Palace of the Embassies next to an illustrious foreigner. His name is Si-ma-teou and he enjoys great prestige at court. His gifts . . ." The Armenian went

175

on to recall the wonders of clocks and spinnets and paintings. "I have a paper here—where is that paper? It is the kind of writing in use among these foreigners. I fetched it with me to show my friends. Here, here is my paper. . . ."

Benito's black eyes flashed with understanding. He saw—it all fit in perfectly! Si-ma-teou was Ricci! Here was proof—there was no Cathay.

XIII

"Abdullah Isai!" Each syllable cracked out, like a pistol shot echoing through a stone chamber. The master of Turfan reloaded and aimed again.

"Abdullah Isai!" he exploded.

"I am here," said Benito, stepping forward.

The sovereign coldly looked down on him and as deliberately measured his spirit. There was a great heart beating beneath that cabaia, he decided. The man was more than a lion—he was a dragon.

"You are about to travel through a country inhabited by Mohammedans," he observed. "It would be more prudent for you to drop the title of Christian."

Behind the master a hundred Mohammedans glared fiercely at Benito. They were ready to cut his throat on the spot and some already had knives in their hands.

"I am going to write down your name. Shall I leave out the word Christian?" the master of Turfan asked.

"Write down that I am a Christian!" de Goes cried out. "It is a title by which I am honored, that I have always borne, and no danger, not even the certainty of death, will make me give it up."

The silence was heavy among Benito's hearers. Sud-

176

denly a venerable old man scrambled to his feet. He jerked off his turban and bowed very low.

"Honor to the faithful believer, to the brave man who dares to avow his faith!" And he bowed low again to the Abdullah.

That night winds swished through naked mulberry branches in Benito's camp-grove. Below, Isaac had his tent and its flap-fabrics rattled sympathetically with the trees. Isaac was not sleeping. He worried and tossed in his blankets till midnight, then crept forth to exorcise his apprehensions with a stroll. As he went out, he quieted the dog with an affectionate pat, then stumbled on a tent-rope. He sputtered impatiently under his breath, searching the sky at the same moment for a moon that wasn't there.

Where will it end, he asked himself. It was perfectly evident that Mohammedans everywhere were determined to squeeze all they could out of the Jesuit. He was legal game and it was open season. How long would he last? Nine months out of Yarkand—he was but a shadow of himself. The mark of doom was on his brow, no mistaking that.

Issac brushed past the camel-drivers' tents. Familiar odors, camels and the unmistakable perfumes of the Orient. The latter were a kind of body-wash to conceal the unpleasant effects of life without bath. Isaac sniffed the fumes indifferently. Redolent of home to him, but for the Brother, wasn't even this a constant reminder of his abandonment?

Now that episode today . . . Isaac could see the palace chamber. All the dignitaries of the desert oasis were there, a row of dour secretaries with pens in hand. The king himself, poised like an inspired Pope in the act of presenting crosses to Crusaders instead of passports to these foreigners. It seemed to be his crowning-day, so solemnly did he nod and appraise his audience. Did he have many such audiences? Not in isolated Mongolia. No wonder he took it so seriously.

Brother Benito should have been killed in that crowd. That is, if the train of events had taken an ordinary course. There was some mysterious charm cast over him. What was it? Others had been bold . . . could it be God?

To what purpose did the great God lead Benito on? Already he knew with a certainty that Cathay was China, that Cambaluc was Peking.

With his mind's eye Isaac again saw the scene in that vast meadow. Two caravans meeting, one from Yarkand, the other from Peking. They share news. They light their fires and crouch around them. Benito has questions. Cathay? Cambaluc? He meets the captain, who has lived with Ricci. The captain has a paper, in Portuguese; Benito, in a flash, understands. He knows for certain there is no Cathay.

Yes, a missing chain-link had been forged that evening in the twilight. Two months ago—Benito for the first time had been loquacious . . . he had acted a little drunk. . . .

Ah, Isaac remembered each detail so well. Benito couldn't sleep. From dusk till dawn he squatted or paced by the campfire, with the captain and the captain's aide, a sullen, buzzard-like merchant with a great hook-nose. Benito talked and talked. His boyhood, his life in the novitiate at Goa, court life with Akbar. Only Isaac understood it all, but the others had listened politely. The captain talked a lot too.

It almost seemed then that Benito would recover from his hardships, not those of the trail, but hardships of the

soul. Isaac sighed. There was the cancer, soul-cancer—
Benito was doomed. Isaac was sure of it, though he
continued to prod embers of the past for some glow of
hope. And he found none before he slipped into his tent
and fell into fitful sleep.

XIV

Turfan, a mere speck on the infinite borders of
Mongolia, presented a pattern quite unlike the oases
farther south. Though Mohammedan, it was more
distinctly Chinese. Instead of the whiskered mid-Asians,
Benito saw now mostly diminutive Mongolian types,
greater numbers of Chinese with small noses, stiff black
hair, and beardless chins.

Benito trotted around Turfan's dusty streets on his
horse, just curious, no longer inquiring about Cathay.
He found a Taoist temple, and in it a hell full of devils
in big green hats. He saw Buddhist monks head-shaved
and skinny, begging for alms that no one seemed to give.
There were Mohammedan mosques, too, several of
them, but no Christian churches.

The weather was intolerably hot because the oasis
was eighty-five feet below sea level in the midst of a
desert and at the bottom of a basin. It was August at that,
the hottest of months, and though the coming winter
would bring sub-zero cold, the promise of a cool autumn
was not even in sight.

It was "grape" weather. Turfan's greatest distinction
among the gardens of mid-Asia was its crop of raisins.
None were finer, and that by the testimony of Khotan's
connoisseurs, who were doubtlessly prejudiced in favor
of their own. Vineyards were plentiful, that is, wherever

there were water-ditches, and to Benito's inexperienced eye, they were the best he had seen. He could imagine vineyards like them on the hillsides of Provence.

The harvest, Benito was told, would be moderate this year. As usual, most of it would go to bandits, "gifts," and taxes. The people would have what was left. They could trade with caravans from the coast for rock-salt, rice, maybe wheat-flour for the rich; or with the moon-faced Mongol camel-hunters from the western desert, who would bring sheepskins for the winter. If the townspeople were lucky, they could get fresh skins. Fresh skins were still greasy, warmer than the best of furs.

Turfan's streets were narrow. They bulged with noisy urchins, bare-legged, earth-blackened creatures with scabs on their faces and running noses and eyes. They scarcely ever smiled except to manifest distrust. When Benito came near, they paused in their quarreling and lice-picking to stare, wise and sad as old people. And when the strange Abdullah held out strips of dried melon for them, they pounced like starved animals.

Benito's stay of a month in Turfan was filled with heartache. Here he was little badgered by zealots of the Prophet, but the poverty, ignorance, and disease of its people almost sickened him. He reached a new low concept of human degradation when he saw young mothers inhale deeply from opium pipes, then blow smoke into the mouths of their new-born babes. That was one way to keep them from crying, even though they were crying for milk.

Everywhere Benito heard talk about bandits. "Beware of bandits!" all said when they heard that the Abdullah's caravan was leaving for the east.

"Your road is called the Road of Three Perils," a

180

withered old man warned him, nodding his head slowly. "Hunger, thirst, and Demons." He counted them off on his fingers. "Hunger is bad. Thirst is worse. But the Demons are worst of all . . . they raise big, big whirl-winds."

"The desert," croaked another, "is possessed by evil spirits. You will hear drums, singing, shrill cries, myste-rious voices. You will see phantoms of all kinds, some one-legged, one-armed, one-eyed. Some will be gigantic, all of them fierce and treacherous. These are the terrors . . . !"

It wasn't with a light heart that Benito started again on a clear September morning. His animals were well rested, even a bit frisky, but there was nothing else to reassure him.

As he passed out of the city gates, he looked back and saw four bandit heads nailed to the wall by their ears.

"Beware of bandits!" the gatekeeper called merrily, noticing the Abdullah's dismay.

Beware of bandits!

It was about two hundred and fifty miles to the next travel-break, and a pair of murders had been reported for every mile. A grim record. Corpses along the trail were a commonplace, usually gruesome sights. Bodies stripped, greenish mummy-like shapes, dried to a half-size underneath the scorching sun, eyes pecked out by vultures. Great caution was necessary to escape a similar fate.

That he might avoid a surprise attack, Benito ordered his horsemen to follow the crests of ridges and sand-dunes, a technique used earlier on the journey. In the more remote regions they travelled only at night. Bronze bells were hung around the necks of several camels which led the procession into the blackness. Others followed by sound, the soft tinkling coaxing them reluctantly along a bitter trail.

After five nights out, Benito tumbled from his horse and was so stunned by the fall that he lost consciousness. In the blackness, no one noticed his absence, not till hours later when Isaac discovered his horse with the saddle empty.

Full of anxiety Isaac retraced his steps, not knowing where to look or how to keep the trail. By merest chance he came to a point where he heard groaning and an anguished voice calling "Jesus." He found his master dragging himself feebly along.

Already Benito had given up hope of regaining his companions and was reflecting on death. It would be a terrible one from thirst, he thought, but welcome for its hope of surcease.

Isaac laid the injured man over the rump of his horse, like a sack, and started to look for the others. By now the sun had appeared and from this Isaac knew only the general direction they had been moving. He would have to take a chance. There was no other way.

For several hours they jogged along dreary gravel-colored hills and sand. Benito was only half-conscious and he moaned now and then while Isaac prayed like an aroused monk. There wasn't the vaguest sign of the trail. And then, just when Isaac least expected it, he saw an obo, rock trail-marker. Fresh tracks were near and Isaac knew they were saved, unless bandits got them first.

He found a water hole surrounded by rocks to keep out the sand, and here he bathed Benito's wounds. With a rag torn from his own shirt he squeezed drops of water down Benito's throat. And then they took off again. Beware of bandits! Isaac remembered. Especially near water holes.

By noon they had regained their companions, who had pitched camp on the banks of a desolate salt-marsh. Benito was put to bed on a rug in his tent, and Isaac, still fasting, hovered over him till he revived.

Another night and day of anxious waiting were spent by the salt-marsh. Then the caravan started again, with Benito in the lead and Isaac at his side.

On the seventeenth of October, 1605, Chami appeared, a little town so full of peace and quiet that Benito stayed by choice a whole month.

X V

When Benito prepared to leave Chami, Agi-Afis had not yet caught up with him. Now this, Benito would have to admit, could be matter for regret. To face the Gobi, the terrible Gobi, he could well use Agi-Afis and his seventy-two ambassadors.

That the smaller caravan had survived Asia's great terrors, like the Road of Three Perils, might be reason for self-congratulation, but it gave no assurance whatever that the good fortune would hold out. To face the Gobi, one needed more than good fortune, for the Gobi was not only a culmination in a series of obstacles, but it was a fitting culmination, a climactic finale of deserts which stretched in a prodigious blight across the Old World. To the Oriental it was *the* desert, the most terrifying of the many deserts of Asia.

Benito undertook this formidable hurdle in November and early December. He wasn't bothered much with "heat," but the icy blasts sweeping down from Siberia were as bad, maybe worse. He had equipped his party with furs, tolerable wraps, and his camels had grown their own furs: they were Mongolian camels. No one froze to death. But, as for comfort, they might as well have been sitting on the Humboldt Glacier in Greenland, which was ten thousand miles away and as cold as a polar frost. The Mongolians of the North Gobi lived in collapsible yurts, wheelless, unlike the yurts of the Kirghiz, and they managed to stay warm even on the frostiest days of winter. Benito had none such refinement; he had a tent and his companions had tents. They lived in them for some thirty days on the cold, windy Gobi.

But the journey, since it was only four hundred miles, finally did come to an end, and that without mishap. On a bleak December day a cold, cold Abdullah, his cold camel-boys and servants and his cold animals arrived at the town of Chia-yu-kuan beside the Jade Gate of China's ponderous wall. The Abdullah and his retinue stood without and waited for admission.

While others routed out officials, the Abdullah gazed around the approaches, idly, without seeing. He chatted affectionately with Isaac. When he talked this way, he was no longer the Persian merchant, Abdullah and lord of a small host of servants. He was Brother de Goes as before, Jesuit momentarily revived, till the curtain rolled back and the act took up again.

This, he confided, was the great moment of his life. China, Old Cathay, lay beyond those hoary walls. Journey's end. Ricci, a brother-Jesuit, awaited him. But most of all—Jesus Christ in the tabernacle!

Had anything on the trail been more difficult than the absence of the sacraments? Nothing! For three long years—they seemed like three hundred—no Mass, no Holy Communion, and no Confession. Not even church

184

or altar, but only idols and temples dedicated to devil-gods and prophets.

A wave of longing trapped him like a beach derelict and flooded his soul. His lip stiffened and quivered. He struggled against the tears, but his heart was bleeding. There was no relief save in yielding.

XVI

Chia-yu-kuan was one of the most celebrated gates in a celebrated Wall. It was at the extreme northwest of the Empire, a pass in the wall-fortress built as protection against the Tartars of Outer Mongolia. Though Chinese characters engraved across the arch read in effect "Barrier of the Pleasant Valley," the site came to be known simply as the Jade Gate, for reasons not difficult to discover.

In the environs of Wall and Gate a frontier town had developed, mostly to supply caravaneers with accommodations till their passports arrived from the Provincial Governor, one hundred and twenty miles distant. The town was really two, one for Chinese, the other for foreigners. By day business was carried on between them, but as soon as the sun had set, all by law kept to their respective quarters.

The Chinese existed at Chia-yu-kuan for the traveller. Rather, from the Chinese viewpoint, the traveller existed for the Chinese, who waxed wealthy (and wise!) from their stranger-victims. Since it was a frontier settlement, there was again this matter of passports and, of course, gift-making. The Chinese wished nothing better than to help their struggling merchant-neighbors, for a price. They would arrange all business with the Palace in

185

Peking, all dispatches, all passports. Why, for a price, they would even forge embassy-credentials of any country. Of any make-believe country! Just pay the price, everything would be taken care of.

De Goes soon discovered that the price was quite beyond his means, despite the jade, and he was reduced to begging a passport as a friendly concession. This favor, very little and yet very great, was not forthcoming; and Benito was left to cool his heels where he was, outside the Great Wall.

While he waited, news of Peking sifted through. The Foreign Devil Si-ma-teou was still the rage in the capital city. He had great influence with the emperor. He had converted a small number of the elite and had won over to benevolence, if not to Christianity, a larger group of powerful lords.

The emperor was in good health, Benito's informers said, but he was nearly overcome with a most untraditional longing. He wanted to look upon the Foreign Devil Si-ma-teou with his own eyes, which gratification tradition strictly forbade him.

After nine days, de Goes finally persuaded the authorities to allow him to proceed as far as Su-chou, about twenty-five miles inside China. It was as far as he ever got.

Like Chia-yu-kuan, Su-chou was a double, a two-town place, one for natives and one for foreigners. The latter was practically Mohammedan, and here the persecution against the Christian Abdullah took up again in earnest. Benito had nothing more to dread from Turkestan or Tartary, cold, hunger, or thirst. He found himself in the midst of urbanity and a suave, omnipresent courteousness. He enjoyed the comforts of civilization, and a hearth of his own. But more than ever he was at the mercy of polished robbers and fanatics. Along with Isaac they were but two against fifty-thousand.

He had arrived at Su-chou with five servants and thirty pack animals, his jade—what was left of it—and some twenty bales of assorted Yarkand products, like cotton fabrics and certain potions for medicine. That sounds like a prince's fortune, but for a man in the role he was playing, it was not enough. If only he could get word through to Father Ricci, he would make it yet.

He dispatched a letter to Ricci as soon as he was able. Would Father Ricci obtain for him a safe-conduct from the emperor? If this were impossible, perhaps the Father could send additional funds for bribing. He didn't like to bribe, he explained innocently, but it was the accepted thing and, usually, nothing else produced results.

At best Benito could expect an answer in five or six months; so he sold his animals, paid off four servants, and with a fifth and Isaac moved into an apartment. All around him now were Mohammedans of every nationality. They harangued him constantly, each swearing loudly in his own tongue, all determined to convert him to the Prophet, or have his skin as a more acceptable alternative.

An exception to this conspiracy of intolerance was Hassan the landlord. A great bull of a man was this Hassan, with a heart as big as his head. He was gusty like a March day. His blowing came in great huffs and puffs, and he grunted or groaned between phrases of his speech. And he befriended the Abdullah against all opposition and that was nobility of the most delicate kind.

Hassan carried his head a little forward and down, so that his crop of black, ill-kept hair was the first part of his anatomy one saw. As the head got nearer, its features delineated somewhat, at least two eyes, the nose, and chin could now be discerned from the mop and flabby mass of fat under it. The eyes, deep and beady, glistened out like bright candies sunk in a steam-pudding. Below them in the middle, a round bulbous nose protruded self-consciously, something like a blister, though not so neat or shapely. And the chin—well, the chin almost lost itself in another, a neck-chin, leaving just a bare suggestion of the curve nature had given him.

It was rumored in the lodging that Hassan put in long hours at the tea-table. There were also reports, more or less substantiated, that great quantities of delicacies from the far away coast found their way to his quarters and disappeared there. Shark-fins, sea-slugs, dog sausages, and bamboo shoots arrived by the camel-load and were turned over to Hassan's Chinese cook. Also kaoling spirits in wondrous volume.

Of course, no one openly said that Hassan consumed all these consignments. It was well known that he dabbled in trade. Maybe the sea-slugs and the kaoling spirits were the items he bartered; at least no one could *honestly* say otherwise, despite the fact that the lodge-keeper's girth increased by weeks.

Whatever his vices, Hassan was a devout Moham-medan. His brand was Afghan, and that was one of the best, at least for getting the most out of life and Paradise too. He had one kind of peeve which was summed up in the word "Cafares," "Unbelievers!" Infidels of the pig! He took this peeve seriously, so seriously that he had got himself a parrot and had trained it to say, "O infidel of the pig, my spittle be upon you!" Whenever he tapped on the parrot's cage, he got the refrain he wanted. "O infidel of the pig, my spittle be upon you!"

Hassan made the distinction between an infidel of the pig and an infidel of the book. Since Benito was in the latter category, he did not merit the old gentleman's opprobrium. Nor the parrot's. And all three got along famously.

"Elder Brother," Hassan would say, using China's title of deference, "you are the friend of my heart. You also worship one God only. We will not quarrel."

And other times, when Benito was particularly harassed by Mohammedan treachery, Hassan would say, "Elder Brother, take heart. My friends admire your courage. They envy only your possessions."

Hassan could not be indifferent to Benito's anxiety. He accompanied the Abdullah in an interminable round of visitations to authorities.

"Remember," he often said, "in Asia, one good present is worth a thousand passports."

Though Hassan had influence with the mandarin, he could do nothing for the Abdullah. It was all a matter of presents. Were there presents? Small presents! Ho! now, the Abdullah could do better.

Only Benito realized how little there really was for presents. The jade was slowly disappearing, not all of it with Benito's consent.

"Do you play mah jong?" Hassan once asked.

No, the Abdullah knew nothing of mah jong.

"A pity," said Hassan.

The Abdullah wondered why it was a pity.

"You see, Elder Brother," said Hassan, "mah jong is a game for soldiers and travellers in China. For soldiers to waste time, for travellers to get passports. When one wants to offer a bribe, he does not say: Here are fifty ounces of silver. He says: Let us play mah jong. And he loses fifty ounces. You see, Elder Brother, very simple. It is the custom."

Hassan tapped the cage and his parrot (called "One-

Eye" because it had lost an eye in its fighting days) croaked obligingly, "O infidel of the pig, my spittle be upon you!"

Hassan and Benito often discussed the tribes of men beyond the Gobi.

"Not tribes of men," Hassan would correct, "Mongols. The Chinese say there are no men beyond the Great Wall. Only Mongols."

Had Hassan remained, the ending of Abdullah Isai's story would probably have been different. In March, three months after Benito's arrival, Hassan retired from business and left with the spring caravan for his native land. Benito, in a burst of self-pity over his loss, or attempting to hurry Ricci's help, wrote him another letter. He didn't know yet that his first had gone astray, and that it would be over a year before help would come.

He was sick, he wrote, but attended by his servant Isaac. He was at the mercy of Mohammedan robbers and mullahs. The local mandarin would not issue him passports. The latter were often promised, but nothing had been forthcoming. His Reverence, Father Ricci, would understand why.

As for Cathay, he had sufficient evidence to prove that it should be identified with China. He had kept a complete journal of his observations and would be pleased to discuss it all with His Reverence.

Would His Reverence hurry the passports from the emperor?

Benito signed his name, "Benito de Goes, S.J." and almost wept over it.

Then he added an afterthought. Some one was filching his possessions, little by little. He had no idea who, nor could he find out. Soon he would be penniless—could His Reverence hurry the passports?

Benito had been sick before, as during the time at Charikar when the caravan left without him. He had recovered both his health and the caravan. Then there was that other time, on the "Roof of the World." That had been a close one, but he got over it just the same. He would get over this too, he told Isaac. A little rest, Isaac's attentions, some feverish blood drained off. . . . He had been drawing on himself for both principal and interest. Now his energies, like certain bank-accounts, were over-drawn.

Isaac wanted to call a doctor from the Chinese zone, a good one whom Hassan had recommended.

No, said Benito, just a week or two. . . .

In June his old companions of the caravan arrived. Six months behind him. They hadn't approved of Abdullah's haste. They suspected him and, besides, he kept a record. In his record were accounts against them, a little bit borrowed here, another bit there. It was quite a sum. Could they get their hands on that account book, or better yet, the jade? Now was their chance, because the Abdullah could muster little courage on his sick-bed.

They were openly hostile. Benito felt it keenly because it was so much more painful than his illness. And as Hassan had gone, there was only Isaac. Time was needed, a little more time. Benito would survive yet.

Weeks faded into months. There was still no news from Peking, nor improvement in the patient's health. He at last consented to see the Chinese doctor recommended by Hassan.

Isaac was overjoyed. Now the master would be cured. Perhaps he would even recover his strong, rugged body which had been so much admired by Asia's little people. He would turn tables on those villainous Mohammedans.

Isaac made elaborate preparations for the arrival of

191

the doctor. Such visits were more like ceremonies in China and every trifling detail must be provided for. He hung out the "doctor's board," a sign that would indicate the sick man's house. He prepared tea and pipes. Then ink and paper and red paper for the "golden thanks," and silver to wrap in the red. After all was ready, Isaac sent a messenger to Tai Hwang Tai Fu, "Dr. Rhubarb."

XVII

Dr. Rhubarb kept office hours till ten in the morning. Then he made his calls around the city.

It was ten now and the eminent doctor announced his intention of leaving. He dismissed a couple, who left with bows and anxious looks at one another, then swirled a silken cloak around him and stepped into the street. His sedan chair was waiting for him; and as he eased into it, one of four coolies tucked his cloak in, then all four of them picked up their burden and hurried it off into crowded and narrow streets.

The coolies were thin-legged and the chair was sumptuously heavy, not to mention the doctor. But their progress, within the hour, was incredible. They had made one call and were already near the foreign devil's place in the foreign quarter. They were slowing down. They came to the lodging where the doctor's signboard was hung conspicuously and they deposited their passenger with a sigh of relief.

Isaac gravely ushered the caller into a reception hall. There were bows, many bows in meticulous observance of the rubrics. Tea and pipes were offered. Dr. Rhubarb pretended to be refreshed. It was time to make the formal request.

192

Would the honorable Doctor Rhubarb feel the patient's pulse? He would. They proceeded to Benito's room. The doctor seated himself beside the bed. He took first the right hand, then the left. He didn't have a timepiece. He just sat and pondered heavily. No questions were asked, for the pulse would reveal all there was to know.

Ink and paper were now produced. Dr. Rhubarb wrote the prescription in doses big enough for a plowhorse. He retired to the reception hall, where he was given his fee wrapped up in red paper—the "golden thanks." Isaac followed him to the door. Again there were bows, and more bows. Isaac paid the chair-bearers their fees, and the doctor was whisked away, giving as his parting benediction a professional nod. The patient, he assured them, would soon recover.

But the patient did not recover. Not even after many moons, nor after many doctors had prescribed their cures and foul-smelling potions. Benito had become a shell, a skin-bag of bones. Little Isaac could pick him up now, to move him in and out of bed.

Isaac had come to suspect something too terrible to mention. He was frantic with terror and grief and there was no one to whom he could turn—in all Sou-chou not one single person. Isaac suspected poison.

He didn't know how—that was the agony of it. But he felt sure of it. Brother Benito was being slowly and systematically poisoned. Isaac administered all the food himself. He bought it, cooked it, served it. He fetched the water himself. Each time he sampled it for taste. He kept constant guard over Benito's bedclothes and blankets. He sniffed at the air for fumes. There was no evidence that he could see, yet he was sure of it. Brother Benito was dying of poison.

193

What would Father Pinheiro have done in this case, Isaac asked himself. He thought of Lahore's genial pastor, "The Mogul," with a tinge of regret. Would Father Pinheiro have told the doctors? Or would he know whether the doctors were part of the conspiracy?

Little Isaac did not know. He only knew that he could not tell the Brother. The Brother was already worried enough.

In his weakness, Benito had got lonely and depressed. Never before had he faced his dangers from this position. A gloom had settled over him like a lethal pall. He tried to steel himself against an overwhelming sense of futility, the feeling of waste, the reflection that he had cast his life away and that there was no finding it again.

Even God seemed to elude him. Like before, in his novitiate days, when God hid behind His gifts of frustration, and emptiness. Was God hostile too, like the Mohammedan merchants? Was God after the "accounts," robbing him of all the kernels of merit, leaving him only the husks of blame? Impossible. God was just, whatever His designs for desolate souls. There would come a time when He would fill what He had emptied, of this Benito was certain even though he couldn't see the hope of it. When that time came, the darkness of night would be dispelled by flashes of God's mercy.

XVIII

If there was any one circumstance that made life difficult for Father Mathew Ricci, it was the brevity of day. In Peking, as elsewhere, twenty-four were but half enough for a man with Ricci's occupations.

He was, first and last, superior of all Jesuits in China:

194

he had many duties to attend to besides entertaining the mandarins, who were as inquisitive as the jays they resembled in plumage, with their gaudy frocks surmounted by dark, sharp-featured heads. As superior, Ricci was responsible for the direction of other Jesuits, Jesuit property, reports to Rome, and so forth, and the constant appeasement of Chinese officialdom. His personality greatly lent itself to these labors. He was gentle and courteous, the perfect type of Roman easiness and affability. His whole bearing bespoke wisdom. All his life he had lived under an influence of books, and this now radiated from him like a kind of holiness.

Father Mathew had acquired a strange reputation for wizardry among the Chinese literati. They said he was an alchemist who could change base metals into gold, and for reasons apostolic, Ricci neither affirmed nor denied this startling magic. The so-called wizardry served as a bait. As such, it drew to him hosts of influential Chinese who would otherwise be beyond his reach. They came at all hours and this was what complicated matters.

Many poured into his lodgings under the imperial acacia trees just to see the "Yang kuei" and his foreign curios. Others were drawn by his theories in memory training and others wanted to hear his discourses on mathematics, cosmology, and religion. They came from all provinces, from all walks of life, for all kinds of reasons. The "Yang kuei" had become a national emergency.

Above all else, Ricci was interested in his Chinese studies: China's literature as well as its languages, Chinese cosmogony, politics, economics, geography. It was the latter that had drawn him into the dispute over Cathay's present status.

What Ricci thought on the subject was well known, for he was never given to reticence. Though he differed with Father Jerome Xavier, he welcomed Xavier's proposal for a mid-Asian expedition, first to prove his own contention, so that the question would be forever settled, and secondly, that the possibilities of a land-route from India to China might be fully appraised. When news came to him that a Brother was on his way via Turkestan and Tartary, he rejoiced as any adventurous Jesuit might and cast his sights on the trail from the west.

For several years now Ricci had waited. He had duly received India's reports on progress made, notice of delays, of Father Machado who was still at Agra, and the Brother's start from Lahore. There had been later reports gleaned from de Goes' first letters to the Provincial and passed along with other bits of hearsay. For example, there was that mystery of Akbar's jewels.

Akbar's jewels had turned up in Agra, in a disreputable bazaar there. When a dealer recognized them, there was the devil to pay. Some one had to go to jail, but no number of shake-downs could produce the Abdullah, who had gone off so gaily with the jewels in his turban. Akbar was left to speculate on the fate of his friend, while Jesuits increased their prayers so that the Abdullah might rejoin them.

On November twelfth, 1605, Ricci wrote to superiors in India that he had heard nothing from central Asia, though he had questioned every visitor who arrived in Peking from those parts. He went on to say that he was convinced more than ever that China was Cathay, and that he hoped soon to have incontestable proof of this.

Ricci would not have fretted so much for de Goes if he were sure the Brother was dead. Death by violence was a rather normal thing in Eastern provinces of the Society. But perhaps de Goes was captive, a slave, mistreated, tortured even. Father Mathew could picture all sorts of appalling trials, and he was troubled exceedingly.

Such was the state of his mind when he was called one day in November, 1606, to receive an insistent "merchant" who claimed to have an urgent message for him. Ricci was accustomed to receive "urgent messages," so he was neither surprised nor alarmed till he saw his visitor.

The man was like a mirage, something too primitive to appear in sophisticated Peking. He might have been a shepherd, God knows from whence. His apparel was a patchwork of hanging things, some of it sheepskin, and his shoes looked like camels' feet, for the simple reason that they were, horny nails, pads, and all. There was but one mark of civilization about him: he wore a scimitar stuck fiercely in his sash.

"You are Si-ma-teou?" said the Mirage, after he had made the ritual bow. He spoke in Chinese.

"I am."

"I have a letter to be delivered to you and no other." He held it out.

Ricci bowed and took the thin packet. He opened it up to determine his correspondent. "De Goes!" he exclaimed. "And from whom did you get this?"

The Mirage had already slipped silently away. There was only a letter to suggest that he had ever been present.

Ricci seized upon his news. The Brother was in Souchou! When was this? Ricci looked at the bottom—Easter Sunday, 1606. The Brother was sick, but attended by his servant Isaac. He was at the mercy of Mohammedan robbers and mullahs. As for Cathay, he had sufficient proof that it was the same as China. Could Father Ricci obtain passports from the emperor?

Ricci planned a relief expedition at once. He sent for a young Chinese, who had but lately pronounced his vows as a Jesuit, a certain Brother John Fernandez, to use the westernized name.

Very minute instructions were given Brother Fernandez. Haste, above all, was necessary. De Goes was ill, perhaps dying. A Jesuit should be at his side with all dispatch, to bring him the comforts of his Order. Expense did not matter. Bribe generously where expedient. Take a number of companions. Deliver the enclosed passports and letters to de Goes and him only. If possible, bring the sick man with his servant Isaac to Peking. If this were not possible, remain with him till he could travel and escort him to Peking with all care and haste. Was this clear?

It was.

Then God be with Brother Fernandez and let him keep in mind that he was racing against time.

Fernandez gathered his needs and set out December eleventh with several Christian neophytes and great eclat. All went well till the party reached Si-ngan-Fou, capital of another province. Here opportunity proved irresistible for one of the neophytes (for him who kept the common purse), and he took leave of the rest without farewells, but with the purse.

Fernandez was stranded and he had no money. He had only his wits left and with these he had to accomplish the near impossible, travel in China without chips for mah-jong.

Ricci had chosen the right man. With labor, arguments, cajoling, and his own bright personality Fernandez charmed his way to Sou-chou, where, despite his ill-luck, he landed in March, 1607. He was a single month behind his scheduled arrival.

In Sou-chou he impatiently paced the streets, inquiring everywhere for a foreign merchant who went by the name of Abdullah Isai. Had the market-keepers of meat and herbs heard of Abdullah Isai? He passed along open stalls where cooks were juggling steaming noodles. Had the cooks who juggled steaming noodles heard of the foreign merchant Abdullah Isai?

The cooks who juggled steaming noodles had heard of many foreign merchants. They regretted to say that Abdullah Isai was not among them.

The answer never varied, not a single syllable.

XIX

There was not much cheer in Sou-chou's Inn of the Camel-Carts; there was desperate business to be tended, ugly business under the sign of the evil dragon. It did not concern China, nor the Son of Heaven, nor were there Chinese in attendance.

It concerned Abdullah Isai, who had committed the unpardonable crime of entering China's Jade Gate with possessions and an accurate account book.

Four merchants sat and smoked in the Inn of the Camel-Carts.

"That Armenian Isaac knows too much," said the first one.

"Strangle him!" said the second.

"No! when the foreign devil dies, Isaac will go to jail," said the third.

The fourth said nothing. He sat motionless, impassive as a carved Buddha.

199

"What about the account books?" said the first.

"I will take care of the accounts," said the third. His eyes were slits of vengeance. His face was cast in a mechanical smile, less of indulgence, more as a mask. "Asia, my friends, has the power of poisoning those who bite it."

X X

March winds were whipping the shutters of his room with rude insistence, and Benito listened disconsolately, wondering whether it made any difference if the clumsy things broke altogether. He called to Isaac to come tie them; but when Isaac appeared, he forgot what he was going to say. It was typical of him these days. He would have something to say and forget it before someone came to listen.

Sometimes when his mind wandered, he was back again in that little church by the shore. Sometimes he was back in the novitiate chapel at Goa, pronouncing his vows again, "perpetual poverty, chastity, obedience." It was strange that the landmarks of his Jesuit life should be so deeply impressed in his memory. Or were they? He could remember them well because he liked remembering. There were other things, less pleasant in retrospect, that he preferred to forget.

"Is there no news?" he said to Isaac. The shutters were still banging.

Isaac said no, but he was sure that some would come. Neither believed it. It was just easier to pretend.

Benito recalled the shutters. Would Isaac tie them down lest the landlord complain?

Isaac would. Was there anything else?

Nothing.

After Isaac had gone, Benito reached for his crucifix. He knew he was dying. He hungered for his own, Fathers and Brothers to whom he had been drawn so closely in his first years of Jesuit life. He hopefully clung to all that was left him: his crucifix. He fingered the cold, hard little figure riveted to the cross-bars, and this was balm for his heart-ache. He was not alone after all. God was with him. God had spoken to him through the command of his superior. This had been his mission, to discover, and in doing so, to bear Christ into the darkness. Who could tell what seeds he had planted, what trails he had blazed in this ancient world that was perishing with him?

Dying, yes. Despite his crucifix, forsaken. No one to bring him the last holy sacraments. No litanies for the dying. Indeed, he knew now that Christ's forsaken hour was the supreme agony in all His sufferings. He had often heard of Father Francis Xavier dying like this on Sancian, of countless other Jesuits, forsaken and buried in unnamed graves. There was an emptiness in lonely death, a soothing emptiness like participation in mysteries. It was, he knew, a seal of approval. No memory stirring within him brought him so close to Christ and his brother Jesuits.

He folded his hands composedly, resignedly. In this last struggle he would not weaken. He could not lose faith now after having lived by it so long, so arduously. Let the Master but summon him. He was ready.

On the last day of March, Benito called Isaac in a thin, tired voice.

"Go to market," he pleaded. "Buy food and give it to the poor. Inquire in the bazaars for a message. Help

201

. . ." he whispered this very solemnly, ". . . help has come from Peking."

Isaac scratched his head and blinked in amazement. Was the good Brother delirious? Help has come—what could he know about this? But humor the sick he must. He pocketed his purse and moodily trudged to market.

Within the hour Isaac was back. He tiptoed to Benito's room, took a peek, then waggled to a shadow at the door. The stranger crept in. He winked at Isaac, then began to read in Portuguese, in a low Chinese sing-song voice, the greetings from Father Ricci.

Benito understood—a Jesuit had finally come! He looked up into Brother Fernandez' face and pressed him to his heart while tears plowed down his wrinkled cheeks.

"Now dost thou dismiss thy servant in peace," he sobbed.

Brother Fernandez placed the packet of letters from Ricci into Benito's hands, and Benito trembled as he opened them. Over and over he read them and kissed them in delight. "See, see!" he cried. "Father Mathew agrees. China is Cathay!"

The news was good medicine. Benito revived a little, appearing at first as though he were on the way to recovery. And then he began to sing again. Isaac and Brother Fernandez kept their places beside him day and night. They prayed and dozed and talked in low tones, but no one ate much. There were no visitors. There was no priest. But Benito was happy. He had found peace at last.

"Do you know," he whispered to Brother Fernandez, "God is very good to me. For many years I have not willfully offended Him. . . ."

God was good to Benito.

202

Eleven days after Fernandez arrived, Benito peacefully breathed his last in the arms of his two friends. It was hardly noticed, till after he was gone. Then Isaac's weeping was all that broke the solemn stillness.

On the next day servants carried his thin remains to the grave. Two mourners followed. Lacking a book of devotions, they prayed the rosary. And as they went along, kicking up little puffs of dust, no one looked up or paused in his occupations to comment on death and the hardships of life. For no one but the mourners really cared.

That same night they took Isaac off to jail.

EPILOGUE

THREE centuries have gone. It is Christmas in twentieth-century Sou-chou. Members of the Protestant Inland China Mission are celebrating the holiday in the true English tradition, receiving callers and dispensing Christian cheer with open hands.

There are many natives present and among them a converted Moslem from the foreign quarter. Groups of twos and threes are chatting amiably. There is a sudden lull—one voice is heard by all. The converted Moslem is speaking.

"I must tell you," he says, "about an interesting ceremony my people observe on the sixteenth day of the third moon. They make a pilgrimage to the tomb of the venerable foreigner, who, though not a Moslem, worshipped one God only."

All listen carefully, intrigued by the prodigy of Moslems paying tribute to a dead Christian.

One of the missionaries, a certain Miss Mildred Cable from London, England, asks questions. Who was the foreigner, from whence did he come? And his grave?

"More than three hundred years ago," replies the converted Moslem with almost doomsday solemnity, "a foreigner reached Sou-chou from India, travelling toward Peking. He died here. It is said that the Chinese refused to touch his body and that even Moslems remained aloof. But the mandarin ordered fitting burial."

The speaker pauses to emphasize the hoary passage of three centuries. Like most Easterners he is a born story teller. "This grave, most excellent madame, lies on the edge of the wind-swept Gobi. The name of the venerable foreigner was Abdullah Isai, whom we know to be Benito de Goes. . . ."

BIBLIOGRAPHICAL NOTE

For sources, I am indebted to many who have gone before me. First there is Father Ricci, whose *Commentari della Cina* is an invaluable Asiatic study. It was edited by Father Tacchi-Venturi, S.J., in our own times: *Opere Storiche del P. Matteo Ricci, S.J.* (2 vols., Macerata, Italy, 1911).

More recently Father Pasquale M. D'Elia, S.J., has edited the definitive *Fonti Ricciane. Documenti Originali Concernenti Matteo Ricci e la Storia delle Prime Relazioni tra L'Europa e la Cina* (1579-1615) (Roma, 1949). Any praise of this work falls short; it must be seen to be appreciated. Ricci's account of the de Goes journey, with Father D'Elia's commentary, appears in the second volume. In his notes Father D'Elia gives the Chinese equivalent of all proper names, and then, for good measure, his own map (for him de Goes by-passed Kabul, but took a side trip to Kashgar), amazingly complete to the last detail.

Another work taken from the Ricci source is Father Nicolas Trigault's *De Christiana Expeditione apud Sinas suscepta ab Societate Jesu Ex P. Matthaii Ricci ejusdem Societatis Commentariis* (London, 1616). The eleventh to thirteenth chapters treat of de Goes and the journey, and are a Latin translation of Ricci's Italian version.

A more recent work on de Goes is by Father Henri Bernard, S.J.: *Le Frère Bento de Goes chez les Musulmans de la Haute Asie* (1603–1607), 1934. This is one of a series on Jesuit mission enterprises. It deserves wider recognition. One scarcely ever finds it listed in bibliographies on that fascinating period which is at last coming into its own.

Father Vernan Guerreiro, S.J., gathered his "Relations" very early under the title: *Relacam annal das cousas que fizeram os Padres da companhia de Jesus nas partes de India Oriental* (Lisbon, 1609), which work was translated in part by Mr. C. H. Payne, *Jahangir and the Jesuits* (London, 1930). One large section of Mr. Payne's learned volume is entitled "The Travels of Benedict Goes." But a short time after the "Relations" appeared, Father Du Jarric came out with his *Histoire des choses les plus memorables advenues*. . . . (Bordeaux, 1614), and this, too, was translated in part by Mr. Payne: *Akbar and the Jesuits* (London, 1926).

On the Mogul theme I used other important works, especially Father Anthony Monserrate's *Mongolicae Legationis Commentarius*, edited by Father Henry Hosten, S.J., and published in the original Latin in *Memoirs of the Asiatic Society of Bengal*, Vol. III (Calcutta, 1914). This composition antedated 1590; hence it is one of the earliest sources of Mogul history. Monserrate made the journey from Lahore to Kabul with Akbar in 1584 and is thus able to give us contemporary details of this part of the route de Goes covered. Father Hosten has made another distinct contribution in his "Notes on Brother Benito de Goes," published in the *Journal and Proceedings, Asiatic Society of Bengal*, Vol. XXIII (1927).

Sir Edward Maclagan's *The Jesuits and the Great*

Mogul (London, 1932) occupies a unique place in Indian Jesuitica, and Sir Edward deserves undying gratitude from Jesuits everywhere for this work. His book served me *per longum et latum,* as it evidently has for many another writer on the same period.

Another book which has become a classic is Father Cornelius Wessel's *Early Jesuit Travellers in Central Asia 1603-1721* (The Hague, 1924). The very first chapter of Father Wessel's work is devoted to Brother de Goes and I cannot help but feel that the Brother is the author's favorite among a whole host of Jesuit celebrities. Father Wessel published other articles on de Goes, one in the *Archivum Historicum Societatis Jesu,* Vol. IV (Rome, 1935), "The Grave of Brother Bento de Goes, S.J." This article served as an authentic source for my "Epilogue."

Among later works there is none more significant than Mr. Henri Cordier's edition of Sir Henry Yule's *Cathay and the Way Thither* (4 vols., London, 1915-1916). He devotes a good share of Volume IV to a translation of Chapters XI, XII, and XIII of Tribault's *De Christiana Expeditione apud Sinas.* Mr. Cordier embellishes the translation with copious and erudite footnotes and a map to illustrate the much-disputed passage of de Goes over the "Roof of the World." Cordier's edition of Yule's *The Book of Ser Marco Polo* (2 vols., London, 1929) covers much of the same ground, of an earlier period.

Then there is the Abbé Hue's *Le Christianisme en Chine en Tartarie et en Thibet* (4 vols., Paris, 1857), which treats of de Goes in the fifth chapter of the second volume. The Abbé calls de Goes "Father," thinking perhaps that he was a priest, which he was not. Certain details appear in the Abbé's account which I cannot find elsewhere. Possibly they are original, entirely so, with the distinguished Abbé.

Father Felix Alfred Plattner, S.J., wrote in German his *Jesuiten Zur See,* and this was translated by Lord Sudley and Oscar Blobel and published under the title: *Jesuits Go East* (Westminster, The Newman Press, 1952). Some of Plattner's pages concern de Goes, but the entire book is somehow related to the riddle of Cathay.

Two fine articles have appeared, one by Father J. Brucker, S.J., in *Etudes Religieuses,* Vol. III (1879), *"Benoit de Goes. Missionaire Voyageur Dans L'Asia Centrale* (1603-1607)," a treatment with a geographer's accent; and the second, with an eye to mission history, by Father James Broderick, S.J., in *The Month,* Vol. CLXXV (1940), "Hunting for Cathay: An Episode of Mission History." The latter is in the brilliant Broderick tradition, worthy of a reading especially by reason of its form. A third article, contributed by myself, has appeared more recently in a symposium of Jesuit Brothers, *Better A Day* (edited by John P. Leary, S.J., New York, Macmillan, 1951). This is simply an abbreviated form of the present work.

Among general sources, I used far too many to mention, but there are several which stand out and complete, so to speak, a de Goes bibliography. First there is Father Sommervogel, S.J.'s *Bibliotheque de la Compagnie de Jesus* (Brussels, 1892), Vol. III, Col. 1529-1530. Then there is Father Elesban de Guilhermy, S.J.'s *Menologe de la Compagnie de Jesus Assistance de Portugal* (2 vols., Poitiers, 1867). Another is Father Ludwig Koch, S.J.'s *Jesuiten-Lexikon* (Paderborn, 1934), Col. 710–712; and, finally, Father Joseph Dahlmann, S.J's *Indische Fahrten.* (2 vols., Freiburg, 1908), in which de Goes appears in the second volume, pages 226 and following.

I have left till last a work which for its maps and illustrations has served me in a unique manner. It is Father Athanasius Kircher, S.J.'s *China Monumentis qua Sacris qua Profanis nec non variis Naturae et Artis Spectaculis aliarumque rerum memorabilium Argumentis illustrata* (Amsterdam, 1667). Without taking it too seriously, I have used it to stimulate my imagination for some choice bits of description. If the reader could enjoy this venerable old tome with me, I'm sure we'd both find a new appreciation for the obstacles Brother de Goes encountered—and overcame.

A NOTE ON THE TYPE

IN WHICH THIS BOOK IS SET

This book is set in Janson, a Linotype face, created from the early punches of Anton Janson, who settled in Leipzig around 1670. This type is not an historic revival, but rather a letter of fine ancestry, remodelled and brought up to date to satisfy present day taste. It carries a feeling of being quite compact and sturdy. It has good color and displays a pleasing proportion of ascenders and descenders as compared to the height of the lower case letters. The book was composed and printed by The York Composition Company, Inc., of York, and bound by Moore and Company of Baltimore. The typography and design are by Howard N. King.

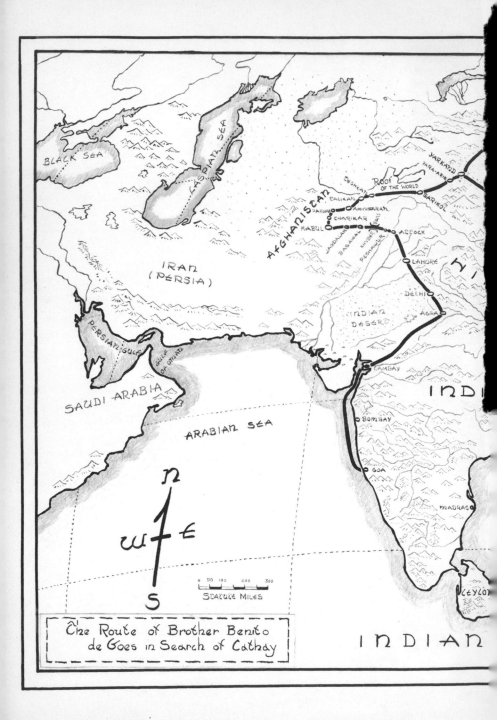

BLACK SEA

CASPIAN SEA

IRAN
(PERSIA)

AFGHANISTAN

Roof
OF THE WORLD

YARKAND
YARA-ARIK

CESHKAT
TALIKAN
SARIKOL

AINISARAH
PARWAN
CHARIKAR
KABUL
JAGDALAK
BAGRAM
KHYBER PASS
PESHAWAR
ATTOCK

LAHORE

DELHI

AGRA

INDIAN
DESERT

HI

PERSIAN GULF
GULF
OF OMAN

SAUDI ARABIA

CAMBAY

INDI

BOMBAY

ARABIAN SEA

GOA

MADRAS

n

w   E

S

CEYLON

0 50 100   200   300
STATUTE MILES

The Route of Brother Benito
de Goes in Search of Cathay

INDIAN